A PRAYER IN THE LIFE

James Whitbourn was born in Kent and educated at Magdalen College, Oxford. Since joining the BBC in 1986 he has worked on a wide range of religious programmes for Radio 2, Radio 3, Radio 4 and the World Service as presenter, reporter and producer. He directed the award-winning drama *The Revelation* which was first broadcast in 1989, and which was played at the 1990 Audio Box Festival in Matera, Southern Italy. He has presented Radio 4's *Prayer for the Day* every Saturday since March 1989. He is married with a daughter, and lives near Sevenoaks.

To My friend Sal

A little book of
comfort, I hope, love ...

A Prayer in the Life

SELECTIONS FROM BBC RADIO 4's
SATURDAY
PRAYER FOR THE DAY

James Whitbourn

TriAngle

First published in Great Britain 1993

Triangle
Society for Promoting Christian Knowledge
Holy Trinity Church
Marylebone Road
London NW1 4DU

British Library Cataloguing in Publication Data
A catalogue record for this book is available
from the British Library

ISBN 0-281-04674-3

Photoset by Rowland Phototypesetting Ltd,
Bury St Edmunds, Suffolk
Printed and bound in Great Britain by
BPCC Paperbacks Ltd
Member of BPCC Ltd

For Alison and Hannah,
with love

CONTENTS

INTRODUCTION

'Of course I remember,' says Cardinal Hume as I reintroduce myself after catching sight of him at the airport in Rome. 'You're the man who ruined my prayer-life!'

It is true the interview had been memorable. It took place in what appeared a quiet and elegant room in Archbishop's House. It was to be a special interview for Easter from the head of the Catholic Church in Britain. The Archbishop's words were deep and thought-provoking. Only when I listened back to the tape did I realize anything was amiss. The whole recording was covered in an electrical hum, which rendered the interview unusable. But not only did the entire programme have to be made again: ever since, says the Archbishop, the faint hum which he had never even noticed before, has seemed to dominate the room he had often used for private prayer.

Radio is a medium full of hazards, but equally full of reward, and there is an extra bonus to be derived from the fact that all the interviews in this book were intended first for radio.

At ten minutes to seven every Saturday morning since March 1989 the BBC has broadcast a conversation on Radio 4 between me and a guest from public life.

When I first make contact with the guests, I ask them to choose a prayer which has inspired their faith. In this context, the word 'prayer' is allowed a much wider interpretation than the formal written prayer with invocation, adoration and petition. The word could describe a scriptural passage, a poem, or any other religious passage of a 'prayerful' kind. It embraces any form of words which allows the guest to turn in devotion, meditation or prayer towards God. I never cease to be surprised by the number of people who know instantly which prayer they would like to discuss. Many people, it seems, genuinely do have a single prayer which has provided an inspiration to their faith.

Except for the special Christmas and Easter interviews, guests receive no prompting from me as to the sort of prayer they should choose. There is no requirement that the prayer should relate to particular events in the news, although often matters of national and international concern crop up. Hence,

1

the interviews in this book include several references to the Gulf War, as well as to events such as the massacre at Tiananmen Square.

On the day of the interview I check my BBC recording equipment. I try to take the sort of equipment which can most easily be forgotten about once the interview is under way, and which allows us a natural conversation. Everything checked, the recorder goes in my bag, and off I go.

Where we meet is up to the guest. Many have invited me to their homes, where we can come to the interview in a leisurely way after a cup of coffee or sometimes lunch. Recordings away from the studio are more fun, though they seem to carry an extra element of risk. People often find that rooms they had thought were beautifully quiet become flooded with noise. It is always dustbin day when I arrive, and the giant mangler is grinding away just across the street. The neighbour's daughter has a piano exam next week, and is earnestly practising her scales. The doorbell goes, the letterbox rattles, the telephone rings, the fridge cuts in. Ticking clocks, cooling radiators and crackling fires are all part of the domestic hazard. And who wants their thoughts on prayer to be fighting against the sound of a blazing furnace?

Before we meet, I have spent time reading and thinking about the prayer myself. I have let it take its effect on me and thought of the sort of questions I might ask. I try never to ask a question to which I already know the answer, and I only ask questions to which I genuinely want to know the answer. We sit down together, each with the chosen prayer in hand. Then comes the surprise.

A scripted talk ensures a well-ordered and logical presentation of a point or argument, but listening to such a talk, you know that the speaker has determined exactly how the sentence will end before he or she begins to talk. With the interview, the reverse is true. Some of the thoughts recorded on tape, and transcribed in this book, are thoughts which have been formulated or developed in the course of a spontaneous discussion, and some of them came as much as a surprise to the contributor as they did to me. They are not necessarily the lines they would have written, had they been asked to contribute to a purpose made collection of devotions, but they are the thoughts which came out on the day.

At the end of the interview, I ask the guest to read the prayer, and I hear it again in a totally different way. I believe this is the experience of many thousands of listeners who tune in every week, many of whom have written asking for a more permanent record than the transient medium of radio can ever provide, of the comments which my guests have made, and the prayers which they have chosen.

I am delighted that I have been able to answer some of those requests through the publication of this book.

No venture of this kind is the work of a single person, and many friends, colleagues and members of my family have made valuable contributions to the programme, particularly by suggesting possible guests. I should like to place on record my thanks to the producers and production assistants who have helped to shape the programme since 1989, especially to Amanda Hancox, who first invited me to present the series, and to Christine Morgan, who took over from her as producer of the series. For their encouragement and guidance I am very grateful.

Above all I should like to offer my sincere thanks to all my guests who have agreed to be interviewed and to share a personal faith not only with me but with thousands of others. In particular, I thank those who have given permission for their interviews and choice of prayers to be included in this book and for those who have sent their good wishes and generous encouragement in the task of putting it together.

James Whitbourn
1993

June, Marchioness of Aberdeen

Haddo House stands majestically in the midst of a huge expanse of woody parkland some way north of Aberdeen. The house was begun in 1731, and it has remained the seat of the earls and marquises of Aberdeen. But Haddo House is also the home of one of Scotland's leading musical bodies, the Haddo House Choral and Operatic Society, begun in 1945 by June, Marchioness of Aberdeen. With its own theatre beside the house, the society stages operatic and concert performances which attract artists of international calibre.

Lady Aberdeen, the society's musical director, lives in an unpretentious but elegant part of the house. You would expect the grace and splendour of the setting to act as a powerful catalyst for the 'serenity' and 'inward happiness' sought after in her prayer. Instead, these are qualities which emerged unexpectedly after her husband's untimely death.

'I was much helped by a Franciscan who was staying here. He said "go out and rail against God! He expects you to." So I let all my horrid feelings out then, in the fields when I was walking. The feeling of resignation came in once I had said what I thought about things. My husband was a very good man, a very beloved man and a deeply religious man, and I could not see why it should happen to him so young. But after I realized that it had to happen, resignation and therefore serenity arrived.'

Following the pattern of the prayer, I ask her to turn her thoughts from inner happiness to its outward manifestation, as 'infectious good courage'.

'I hope I am infectious with good courage. I am jolly frightened very often but I do hope I've got courage in the big things of life. I think it is very important to be able to help other people by the way you live and by your own personal happiness. I think if people see you carrying on in the face of difficulties, they realize that they can do it too. There are moments when it is very difficult to be gallant and show high-hearted happiness. But when the worst has happened, you think "nothing so bad can ever happen again", and, if you are surrounded by good things and the love and affection of friends, you can have a high-hearted happiness without any insincerity at all.

'If I am feeling very low, I shut myself away. That has always been my motto. And right at the beginning, when I was totally devastated and the whole of my life was shattered, I never wept in public. I used to go and cry alone, because I think tears are very private things. But a smile can do so much, and if you smile to people, they smile back, the whole world is at your feet.'

June, Marchioness of Aberdeen and Temair. Musical Director and Conductor, Haddo House Choral and Operatic Society (formerly Haddo House Choral Society), since 1945.

Grant to us,
Lord,
the royalty of inward happiness
and the serenity which comes from living close to thee.

Daily renew in us the sense of joy,
and let thy Spirit dwell in our hearts,
that we may bear about with us the infection of a good courage,
and may meet all life's ills and accidents
with gallant and high-hearted happiness,
giving thee thanks always for all things;

through Jesus Christ, our Lord.

Richard Adams

'It is the basis of Christianity, I think.'

The best-selling author examines the brief lines of the Collect for the Sunday before Lent, adapted for Cranmer's Prayer Book from St Paul's epistle to the Corinthians. The language of the prayer is uncompromising and unapologetic, and its message is bold. Yet the exact nature of 'charity', the gift which is central to the understanding of the prayer, is strangely hard to define. Some people call it 'love'. What does Richard Adams mean by the word?

'In this context I would render "charity" in modern usage as "a kind heart". It is loving the world and the people in it, not entertaining hatred, resentment or envy of any other person, and being always on the look-out to do a kind action.'

To use the words of Cranmer's prayer, charity is also the very bond of peace and all virtues. So how does charity pull together all other gifts?

'Actually the trick of the thing has been used before by Aristotle. Aristotle says that all the virtues are no good without courage, and without it you cannot practise any of the others. What the prayer is saying is that without a kind heart, you are no good. It is like the cement which sticks the bricks together, or the salt in the stew. You have to have a kind heart, and that will render all other things effective.

'Thinking about people you deal with in everyday life, you can very quickly discern whether a person has what you would call "a kind heart". And I do indeed believe that is quintessential, and was exemplified by Jesus Christ himself throughout his life, not only in his teachings but in his actions. The Good Samaritan did not just pick the man up, he tended his wounds, took him to the nearest inn, paid the bill and left a deposit. He left nothing lacking at all. He goes out of his way to emphasize the glorious nature, the generosity and magnanimity.

'I believe entirely what the prayer says, that if you have not got the quality you are praying for, you are counted dead before God. It is quite a statement, when you come to think of it. And I entirely agree with the whole tenor of the prayer, which I think sums up the intrinsic nature of Christ's gospel and Christ's teaching.'

Richard Adams, Author. Novels include: Watership Down, *1972;* Shardik, *1974;* The Plague Dogs, *1977;* The Girl in a Swing, *1980;* The Bureaucrats, *1985;* Traveller, *1989.*

O Lord,
who hast taught us
that all our doings without charity are nothing worth:
Send thy Holy Ghost,
and pour into our hearts
that most excellent gift of charity,
the very bond of peace and of all virtues,
without which whosoever liveth
is counted dead before thee:

Grant this for thine only Son Jesus Christ's sake.

The Collect for Quinquagesima, or the next Sunday before Lent,
The Book of Common Prayer (1662)
(based on 1 Corinthians 13. 1)

Kriss Akabusi

'I am one of those people who really does believe that my talent has been God-given, and I think that God gives everyone on this earth a particular talent.'

There is no denying the talent given to Kriss. Our meeting comes just before he flies out to Barcelona for the 1992 Olympic Games. He is to return a medal-winner, after breaking his own British record in the fastest 400m hurdles race ever run.

'God has helped me find my talent and develop it', he explains.

Kriss is doing his bit too. We have found a corner in one of the quieter rooms of the new, rubber-smelling sports hall, where the hard work behind the glamorous Olympic track gets done. But even the nation's expectations of the world's most glorious and prestigious games are overshadowed by the words of Psalm 8.

'The psalm speaks about the glory of God and the majesty of God, and I think it is a great way to start any prayer or any discourse with God. It is to highlight his magnificent glory, and how far and wide he supersedes anything you can conceive on earth.

'When I see the position that I have, as a person in the human race in the line of God's creation, I feel crowned. Crowned because I have dominion over all the earth, and that is such an awesome position to be placed in. Then I realize that God himself came down to earth, that he lowered himself, from the high majesty that he had, to be a little lower than the angels, and on the same level as me. When I read that and think of what God has done for me, it is absolutely terrifying.'

Does the knowledge that God places such trust with mankind change the way you look at people?

'Before I became a Christian, I saw a hierarchy of people, and I was at the lower end of that hierarchy or social scale. Now, in becoming a Christian, I realize that God made each and every one of us the work of his hands, and we are made equal in the sight of God. That certainly changes the way I interact with people. Regardless of what they are, on a social or economic scale, I realize that, if God loves them, how much more should I love them. So in that respect life has changed and given me, I think, a higher opinion of myself. I realize that, regardless of what sort of accent I speak with or of what sort of colour I wear, we are all equal in the sight of God.'

Kriss Akabusi. British athlete. Medals include: 1984 Olympics, silver (4 × 400m relay); 1992 Olympics, bronze (400m hurdles): bronze (4 × 400m relay); 1987 World Championships, silver (4 × 400m); 1991 World Championships, gold (4 × 400m): bronze (400m hurdles).

O Lord,
our Lord,
how majestic is your name in all the earth!

You have set your glory above the heavens.
From the lips of children and infants you have ordained strength*
because of your enemies,
to silence the foe and the avenger.

When I consider your heavens,
the work of your fingers,
the moon and the stars,
which you have set in place,
what is man that you are mindful of him,
the son of man that you care for him?
You made him a little lower than the heavenly beings
and crowned him with glory and honour.

You made him ruler over the works of your hands;
you put everything under his feet:
all flocks and herds,
and the beasts of the field,
the birds of the air,
and the fish of the sea,
all that swim the paths of the seas.

O Lord,
our Lord,
how majestic is your name in all the earth!

*or praise

Psalm 8 (New International Version)
(For a different version of Psalm 8, see Bruce Kent, p. 74.)

Metropolitan Anthony of Sourozh

'We have a very deep sense of the mystery of God.'

A depth of feeling moulds every nuance of his speech. With Russia still under Communist rule at the time of our interview, it is still only in exile that the Russian Orthodox Church can live out its tradition without fear. And here, among the icons in the beautiful London cathedral, talking to the head of the Russian Orthodox Church in Britain, is a glimpse of what once had been and, as it turns out, of what is soon to come again.

He speaks slowly now, his quiet, rich and sonorous voice, pausing now and then to let silence fill the cathedral.

'In order to be in harmony with God we must be open to him and listen deeply so as to hear from the depth of his silence the word which is truth and which is life.'

The prayer speaks of 'worship in silence', and begins with an admission of the inadequacies of human understanding both of ourselves and of God. But it raises the question of the value of prayer, given the ignorance of what we ask.

'I think that any reasonable person knows that he knows himself very little, and so when we stand before God we want to present to him all that is true in us, our needs, our hopes and our love. But all these things we discern as though it were through a fog, and so we say to him "in whatever is mistaken, act according to thy wisdom, and not according to my folly".'

The prayer demands first that people should open their hearts to pain and hurt, before they ask of God 'pray thou thyself in me'. Is this a question of total submission to God?

'I think one should be able to open one's heart to pain and hurt. When we trust someone, we are prepared to receive from him or from her both pain and joy, so the openness of which we speak is a sign of our complete trust and of our readiness to put our lives into his hands. To say to God, "pray thou thyself in me" is not a question of submission. It is a question of communion and of the joy of being at one, in the way in which a little twig which was half dead, when grafted on to a life-giving tree, is gradually filled with the sap of this healthy tree and becomes truly itself, although it is filled with the sap which is not of itself.'

Metropolitan Anthony of Sourozh. Head of the Russian Orthodox Patriarchal Church in Great Britain and Ireland (Diocese of Sourozh).

Oh Lord,
I know not what to ask of thee.
Thou alone knowest what are my true needs.
Thou lovest me more than I know how to love myself.
Help me to see my real needs which are concealed from me.
I dare not ask either a cross or consolation,
I can only wait on thee.
My heart is open to thee;
visit and help me,
for thy great mercy's sake;
strike me and heal me,
cast me down and raise me up.
I worship in silence thy holy will and inscrutable ways.
I offer myself as a sacrifice to thee.
I put all my trust in thee.
I have no other desire than to fulfill thy will.
Teach me how to pray.
Pray thou thyself in me.

Russian Orthodox prayer

Mary Archer

'A lot of scientists think in very vivid and imaginative terms. It is only when they have to put down their thoughts in prose that they sober up.'

Dr Archer's words do more than defend the inventive and colourful language of the psalms. She also says something of the working of the scientific mind.

'I am attracted by the opening words to the idea that the very beauty and majesty of the cosmos declares the intelligence of it. The heavens, the universe, the galaxies and all the variety of life on earth are so wonderful, in a scientific sense, that I think they declare their own glory. And when the psalmist then writes, that "one day telleth another, there is neither speech nor language, but their voices are heard", I think he is saying that the bits of the heaven known to him, the planets and the visible stars, are certifying one to the other the glory of their creator. One can imagine the planets wandering among the stars and talking to them. And I like to read into that the mediaeval idea of the "music of the spheres". That is the charming idea that because the radii of the orbits of the planets fall into fairly simple proportions, one to the other, maybe they sing a chord as they move. It is a lovely idea that somehow the movement is accompanied by a sound.'

I cite the verse 'he set a tabernacle for the sun: which cometh forth as a bridegroom out of his chamber' as an example of the unscientific nature of the psalm.

'I like it because the sun has created and sustains life on earth, and it is our most potent symbol of power, warmth and light. And I think the change of scale in the personal prayer at the end of the psalm leads naturally on, because contemplation of the enormity and the majesty of the universe leads one to feel very small in comparison. Astronomers often feel that when they peer down their telescopes. So I think religion is helpful in giving one a proper sense of proportion, and therefore a sense of one's own worth and importance. There is nothing so important as people. If we took that view more widely perhaps the world would be a better place.'

Lady Archer (Dr Mary Archer). Scientist. Fellow of Newnham College, Cambridge, and Lecturer in Chemistry, 1976–86; Trustee, Science Museum, since 1990; Member, Council of Lloyd's, 1989–92.

The heavens declare the glory of God:
and the firmament sheweth his handywork.

One day telleth another:
and one night certifieth another.

There is neither speech nor language:
but their voices are heard among them.

Their sound is gone out into all lands:
and their words into the ends of the world.

In them hath he set a tabernacle for the sun:
which cometh forth as a bridegroom out of his chamber,
and rejoiceth as a giant to run his course.

It goeth forth from the uttermost part of heaven,
and runneth about unto the end of it again:
and there is nothing hid from the heat thereof.

Let the words of my mouth, and the meditation of my heart:
be alway acceptable in thy sight,
O Lord:
my strength, and my redeemer.

Psalm 19.1–6, 14–15
The Book of Common Prayer (1662)

John Banham

'I have always found that a sense of service to others, a sense that you are accountable to somebody and to something beyond yourself, beyond your family, beyond your bank balance, has always been rather important to me in life.'

The Director-General's office towers over the capital, high up in one of the symbols of British commerce. Centre Point serves as the headquarters of the Confederation of British Industry.

'My concern for serving', says Sir John, 'is not at all incompatible with a career in commerce and industry. Quite the reverse. I have always thought that serving other people was the highest form of freedom and the ultimate goal for anyone. Of course, to "serve the Lord as he deserves" is a very difficult task, but, in my experience, nothing is worth doing unless it is difficult. Unless you have very unrealistic ambitions you will never get anywhere. Unless you reach for the moon you are unlikely to get to the end of the road. And I think having an ethical basis for the way one spends one's life is a very important element in almost everybody's life.

'But I think what appeals to me about the prayer of St Ignatius is the notion that you have to stick to what you believe. There are huge pressures in our society to go along with the received wisdom. There are tremendous obstacles to people who say what they believe and stick to it, and you must not expect any rewards. There are no rewards for being right, and, on the whole, people do not want to stand up and be counted. They would rather have their heads well down below the parapet and watch everyone else take the shot and the shell. I find it here at the CBI. It is a very lonely business, and yet we have obligations to ourselves and to our fellow citizens, and we have one higher obligation which is to be honest.

'In the kind of job I do, the real reward is to see things improve, and I think many of us go into commerce because we know in the long run that that is the only way to deliver improved standards of living to everybody. Very many leaders of business are very devout because they have an obligation which goes beyond simply amassing wealth in this life. I certainly feel that.'

Sir John Banham. Director-General, Confederation of British Industry, 1987–92. Chairman, West Country Television Ltd, since 1992.

Teach us,
good Lord,
to serve thee as thou deservest;
to give and not to count the cost,
to fight and not to heed the wounds,
to toil and not to seek for rest,
to labour and not to ask for any reward
save that of knowing that we do thy will.

St Ignatius Loyola
(1491/5–1556)

David Bellamy

'I'm a very emotional person and I can actually cry when I'm saying my prayers; and when I say that part of the prayer it does make me cry.'

Jesus' words in prayer had struck a chord with the television botanist and conservationist: 'Give us this day our daily bread'.

'It does make me cry because fourteen million children are going to die this year of conditions relating to malnutrition. It's no earthly good, unless you want to go to heaven prematurely, not feeding the body as well as the soul.'

The Lord's Prayer, says David Bellamy, is the best prayer he can imagine for a conservationist, and it is a prayer now deeply embedded in his consciousness:

'I was taken to church at the age of three, and I suppose I have said it almost every day of my life since. You went to church and it was there moving through your mind the whole time, and it does say so many important things which have been with me all my life as a Christian. Of all the things, I think it has given me strength. This prayer becomes part of the strength through spirituality, as long as you don't take it as being idle repetition. I have gone through great periods of despair over humanity, and over Christianity, but one always comes back to the fact that you are sitting quietly somewhere and the first thing you say starts off with words of the Lord's Prayer.

'It is a prayer, as you say, which points to the tremendous responsibility placed on humankind: "Thy will be done on earth as it is in heaven". To me, the first responsibility given to humankind, by the first commandment, was to have dominion. I remember sitting with my father, who was quite a Hebrew scholar, going back to find out what the word "dominion" meant. As far as I can see it meant "wise rule". I never had a "Damascus road", I only ever saw the light walking through the Surrey countryside, with the dew and with the toadstools growing, and that, to me, was God's creation. We have got to look after it, and we have got to keep working very hard to make God's kingdom come on earth. I think it is going to be full of animals and plants and creepy-crawlies and wonderful people saying "thank you".'

David Bellamy. Botanist, writer and broadcaster. Special Professor, Nottingham University, since 1987. TV programmes include: Longest running show on earth, *1985;* Bellamy on Botany, *1983;* Bellamy's Bird's Eye View, *1988;* England's Last Wilderness, *1992.*

Our Father,
who art in heaven,
hallowed be thy name;
thy kingdom come;
thy will be done;
on earth as it is in heaven.
Give us this day our daily bread.
And forgive us our trespasses,
as we forgive them that trespass against us.
And lead us not into temptation;
but deliver us from evil.

For thine is the kingdom,
the power,
and the glory,
for ever and ever.

Tony Benn

'I was brought up on the Old Testament. My mother could read the Old Testament in Hebrew and the New Testament in Greek, and the thing she taught me most about the Old Testament was of the conflict between the Kings and the Prophets: the Kings, who exercised power and had a very good time, and the Prophets, sometimes in the wilderness, who preached righteousness. The Prophet Amos, as the great preacher of righteousness, was one of the prophets of whom she spoke, and his word are still in the back of my mind – and sometimes in the forefront of my mind – when the clash between the law and conscience comes to the fore.

'I have always believed that great religions, like progressive political parties (and they have very much in common), begin with a flame of faith and end up with a bureaucracy, with hierarchies and celebrations. That is the point at which the original purpose of the faith is corrupted and diverted. I know the passage itself sounds very puritanical (which I am sure Amos didn't intend, and I wouldn't intend) but I have seen many, many people in my life diverted from a faith by all the luxury of life at the top. I think that is what Amos speaks about in this passage.

'The argument is about the choice you have to take between a man-made law and some inner voice of conscience, and Amos speaks about this idea that everybody has a duty to reflect the sense of justice and righteousness. And if you keep that stream of influence to bear on a society, it will tend to correct the errors. Reinhold Niebuhr, the American theologian, who was a great friend of my family, once said, "Man's capacity for evil makes democracy necessary, man's capacity for good makes democracy possible," and I think that is the balance that Amos helps us to understand.

'There is good and bad in everybody, and I think over the last few years we have been encouraged to stimulate those parts of our nature which are the least desirable. Some evil values have been officially peddled. What Amos is saying in this passage is quite clear: that we have to develop and present, as best we can, a concept of justice and righteousness. That is what politics and religion ought really to be about, and he made it so clear that it is difficult to forget his words.'

Rt Hon. Tony Benn. Labour Member of Parliament. Secretary of State for Industry and Minister for Posts and Telecommunications, 1974–75; Secretary of State for Energy, 1975–79.

[Thus says the Lord, the God of hosts:]

I hate, I despise your feasts,
and I take no delight in your solemn assemblies.
Even though you offer me your burnt offerings and cereal offerings,
I will not accept them,
and the peace offerings of your fatted beasts
I will not look upon.
Take away from me the noise of your songs;
to the melody of your harps I will not listen.

But let justice roll down like waters,
and righteousness like an ever-flowing stream.

Amos 5.21–24
(Revised Standard Version)

Tony Britton

Looking over from the market cross, where the four main roads of Chichester meet, the Cathedral Church stands guard over its small and attractive town. Entering the building, its elegant vaults enclose a warm and intimate space which has been a refuge for worship and prayer throughout most of English history. St Richard Wych, who became Bishop of Chichester in 1245, was the thirty-eighth bishop there. He is probably best known through a single prayer which has become part of Chichester's heritage. Tony Britton remembers reading the prayer at the back of the cathedral, during a moment off from rehearsals in town.

'Chichester has been an extraordinary place for me. It began in sheer and absolute joy and fulfilment as far as my work was concerned. And then, inevitably, certain difficulties began to occur, and I found that this prayer was an enormous help, and the cathedral itself a great solace.'

St Richard begins his prayer with thanks both for all the benefits given, and for the pains and insults which have been borne, which together form what Tony Britton calls a 'circle of light'.

'A little while ago, in the middle of quite a lot of crises of emotion, practical difficulties and stresses of one kind or another, I suddenly realized that at the centre of all this there was a little circle of light which was absolutely undisturbed. And around it, all these fears and anxieties, worries and neuroses were revolving. I realized that all the things that were revolving around this centre of light were totally unimportant, and that the centre of light was always there and is always going to be there.'

The most famous part of Richard's prayer embodies a succinct but powerful formula for Christian discipleship, from the mind to the heart and into action. So how do the knowledge and love of Christ work together with the compulsion to be like him?

'I think that it is a very difficult one to answer, because it is so incredibly difficult to come anywhere near feeling that one knows Christ. Occasionally you find that something you happen to hear suddenly strikes home, and you say, "Ah yes, that's the man". I was reading the Gospel of St John, for instance, and I came towards the end of the story, and Christ asks Peter three times, "Peter, do you love me?", and Peter says, "Of course I do, you know very well I do". Each time Christ says something like "feed my sheep", I find that very moving and deeply human. But it is difficult to get to know someone who lived two thousand years ago, and until you have done that it is very difficult, quite honestly, to say, "I love that person". So it is a very long journey summed up in those three things, to know, love and follow Christ. And I think he summed it up beautifully, old St Richard.'

Tony Britton. Actor. Leading roles in television series include: Don't wait up; Don't tell father.

Thanks be to thee,
O Lord Christ,
for all the benefits which thou hast given us;
for all the pains and insults which thou hast borne for us.

O most merciful redeemer,
friend
and brother,
may we know thee more clearly,
love thee more dearly,
and follow thee more nearly;
for thine own sake.

St Richard Wych (1197–1253)
(Bishop of Chichester, 1245–53)

Peter Brooke

It is another week of brutal sectarian violence in Northern Ireland. The headlines are using the words of the head of the RUC to describe the latest bout of killings in Belfast: 'Murder Madness'. Before flying back to the scene of the murders, the Northern Ireland Secretary keeps an appointment to discuss the prayer used by Sir Jacob Astley before the battle of Edgehill in 1642.

'This prayer was produced by a royalist commander in the field in the very early days of the English Civil War, at a time when the circumstances of civil strife had a degree of religious connotation, and therefore I feel a degree of sympathy with its author. He was asking God to look after him during the course of the day, though he was failing in any more extensive prayer himself.

'I am not a very good pray-er. Not because of any aversion to prayer; I simply make the confession. But I find that it is important, both in the morning and in the evening, to have the ability to speak to God, and the great virtue of this brief prayer is that it is very easy to remember, and it is very succinct as a preparation for the day.

'Astley said it in the context of going into battle. I would not want to so dramatize my life as to imply that I am so engaged. But in the nature of life, combining responsibilities within Northern Ireland and within the government, while at the same time continuing to have responsibilities to constituency and family, one knows that every day is going to be busy. What you can never tell, because of the particular circumstances of this job, is what disagreeable surprises are going to occur, and what unwelcome news will be broken. It is that sense of wishing to keep close to God during the day that underlies the prayer.'

From the outset of our conversation, the Secretary of State had emphasized that he wished to be strictly honest about his experience of prayer. But his own description of himself, as one who is not as regular in his prayers as he would wish to be, seems to tie in so closely with the experience of Lord Astley, who ended his prayer with the plea 'If I forget thee, do not thou forget me'. So can human inadequacy be met with attentiveness from God?

'Any answer would necessarily sound self-centred but there is no doubting the comfort which comes from the sense of consciousness during the day that all is well. And the ability to keep going clearly does not come from within oneself.'

Rt Hon. Peter Brooke. Conservative Member of Parliament for City of London and Westminster South, since 1977. Secretary of State for Northern Ireland, 1989–92. Secretary of State for National Heritage, since 1992.

O Lord,
thou knowest how busy I must be this day;

if I forget thee,
do not thou forget me.

General Lord Astley (1579–1652)
(before the battle of Edgehill)

Eva Burrows

'I was really surprised when I first read this prayer, that in the eleventh century they can have tumults in their thoughts.'

Anselm's prayer was written a few years before he came to England as Archbishop of Canterbury, but already, in his positions as abbot and prior in France, he had had a taste of the violent conflict which was to come with the King of England in the final years of his life.

'I thought the twentieth century was the busiest century,' remarks the Salvation Army General, before casting her mind back again to the tumult which had faced an international Christian leader some nine hundred years before.

'Really, wherever a person is involved with people and seeking to do the work of God, there will be demands, so whatever century it is, there is a time which must be spent with God.

'Each morning, when I rise, I have a time for prayer. Anselm says, "turn aside for a while". He is a man who was obviously very busy in his life as a Christian leader, and he knew that you could not spend long periods in prayer, but that if you could spend a while with God it is so refreshing and so strengthening. I do pray regularly throughout the day with little "arrow-prayers" shot up to God when I am facing an immediate decision, so I feel God with me all the time. But I feel it is absolutely necessary for me to draw near to God first thing in the morning, to sense his presence and to know that he is with me. I find it a necessity. And in that moment when I am with him, I find that his presence fills my whole being.

'The question is how to combine an activist life with a meditative life, and I have never found that very easy. I want to find the balance between involvement and detachment because I cannot face those tumults, those burdens or those distractions without the awareness of God being with me. My favourite saint is St Teresa of Avila, who reformed the monasteries and convents of the post-Reformation period, but at the same time had a very rich contemplative life. I call her a "militant mystic" and I would like to feel that I were something like that.

'The times with God are very important to sustain what I am doing in my active life for him. When Anselm says "escape for a moment", that is not escapism. You do not go there in order to avoid the realities of the workaday world, but to retreat for a moment from the pressures, in order that God may fill your life with his power and grace.'

Eva Burrows. General of the Salvation Army, 1986–93.

Come now, little man,
turn aside for awhile from
your daily employment,
escape for a moment from
the tumult of your thoughts.
Put aside your weighty cares,
let your burdensome distractions wait,
free yourself awhile for God
and rest awhile in him.
Enter the inner chamber of your soul,
shut out everything except God
and that which can help you in seeking him,
and when you have shut the door, seek him.
Now, my whole heart, say to God,
'I seek your face,
Lord, it is your face I seek'.

St Anselm (*c*.1033–1109)
(Archbishop of Canterbury, 1093–1109)

George Carey

'I remember, twenty-one years ago, holding my younger daughter, Lizzie, in my arms as a newborn baby. She was two hours old at that point and I was amazed by her vitality and the life that was in her. This prayer is saying something about being born anew, and when I say it, I am reminded of that experience twenty-one years ago.'

Birth and rebirth is the theme for a special interview to be broadcast on the Saturday before Christmas, 1992. The Collect for Christmas Day reflects on the humanity of God.

'God takes our nature (we therefore give God something) and then God gives us something: he gives us his divine life and his spirit. In my experience, this says it all. When I started out in my Christian life, more years ago than I can possibly remember, it was like being born again. It is God's life flooding our own souls, so that we know that we live our Christian life by the power of God.

'The mystery is that God chooses to come to us to take on a lowly estate himself and to be one of us in order to raise us to the heights of Godhead. It is a mystery, but at the same time the reality is there. This is God's way. Because God invests himself in reality, there is nothing unworthy about this world or distasteful about material things. He gives himself to the world, and so should Christians. We don't pine for heaven: heaven is to be found on earth, here and now, and continues on into eternal life which God gives to all those who are born again in him.

'In John Chapter 1 it says that "he came unto his own, and his own received him not. But as many as received him, to them gave he power to become the sons of God". That is what this prayer is all about.

'It is a mystery, of course, and that is why a lot of people object to the virgin birth, saying "I can't understand it—it's impossible". So they reject it. But a lot of life is mysterious: I find it very mysterious to know how God's life and love can fill me (or any Christian for that matter) and yet we know the reality and joy of that experience. For the Christian, every day is Christmas Day.'

Most Revd and Rt Hon. George Carey. Archbishop of Canterbury, since April 1991. Bishop of Bath and Wells, 1987–91.

All praise to you,
Almighty God and heavenly king,
who sent your Son into the world
to take our nature upon him
and to be born of a pure virgin.
Grant that, as we are born again in him,
so he may continually dwell in us
and reign on earth as he reigns in heaven
with you and the Holy Spirit,
now and for ever.

Collect for Christmas Day
The Alternative Service Book 1980

Roy Castle

"Roy's tiny chance of life." "Too many gigs in smoky clubs." The papers seem to offer little hope. Roy's lung cancer is a rare and severe form brought about through a lifetime of inhaling other people's fumes. Roy takes a more optimistic view. I arrive at his house to find a man in fighting form. He has no hair: that is part of the treatment. He can only walk a few slow steps at a time: that is to be expected too. But the smile is still intact, and the television entertainer is happy to turn his thoughts away from his present troubles. The passage from Paul's letter to the Romans could claim a longer and a deeper influence on him as he reflects on the diversity of talents given to other people and to himself.

'Some people seem to have what you would call an enviable job in life, and other people seem to have an unenviable job. But without everybody doing their bit, society just doesn't work. I consider myself very well blessed because I have a talent which can entertain people and which is very enjoyable to me too. But I know that the gift from God is raw, and you have to work at it and practise and practise, and do the best with that talent that you possibly can.'

There is a striking mixture of talents named by St Paul. Most striking of all is the way in which spiritual gifts, such as the ability to preach or prophesy, intermingle freely with the profane, such as financial or administrative ability. So can any activity be regarded as holy?

'You have to feel in your heart that it is for the good of society and other people as well as yourself, and good to honour God. You have to have this gut feeling that it is right, and you get this from asking God in prayer and meditation. He will never lie to you. So if he says "yes", then you do it to the best of your ability.'

Does the ability to love one another require practice and work just like any other gift?

'I think perhaps it does need consideration. Again, it is that gut feeling: "Am I putting this person down?" "Am I giving them a fair try?" "Am I doing it for my own benefit while they lose out?" We all have a job to do, we have to do it together. And at the end of it all, we must all share the profits. The profits sometimes can just be a very happy feeling. Sometimes it is money, and, if so, good luck!'

Roy Castle. Entertainer/Actor. Films include: Dr Who and the Daleks; Carry on Up the Khyber. *Television series:* The Roy Castle Show; Roy Castle Beats Time; Record Breakers *(presenter);* Castle's Abroad.

God has given each of us the ability to do certain things well.
So if God has given you the ability to prophesy,
then prophesy whenever you can –
as often as your faith is strong enough to receive a message from
    God.

If your gift is that of serving others,
serve them well.
If you are a teacher,
do a good job of teaching.
If you are a preacher,
see to it that your sermons are strong and helpful.
If God has given you money,
be generous in helping others with it.
If God has given you administrative ability
and put you in charge of the work of others,
take the responsibility seriously.
Those who offer comfort to the sorrowing should do so with
    Christian cheer.

Don't just pretend that you love others:
really love them.
Love each other with brotherly affection
and take delight in honouring each other.

Romans 12.6–10
(The Living Bible)

Donald Coggan

'There are perhaps more occasions than not when you have no great feeling of God's presence, but you know very well that he is there.'

I can imagine a sense of profound relief among listeners who will hear these words from a former Archbishop in the provinces both of York and Canterbury. His words spring from a consideration of a well-loved prayer from the end of the Eucharist in the Anglican Rite A liturgy. It is a prayer full of imagery, which draws on the words of the writer of Hebrews and on Christ's description of divine love given in the parable of the Prodigal Son. Has Lord Coggan been met like the prodigal son?

'Not in a dramatic way. No startling conversion just like that. But down a pretty long life I have known, again and again, of the way that God meets with us, and gives us strength, insight and understanding when we feel we lack those things. After all, the prodigal son's father went out to meet him long before the son had plucked up courage to come home. The wonderful thing about God, as Jesus revealed him, is that he is the first to move towards us, long before we move towards him. Constantly he comes to us through communion with him in the sacrament that our Lord instituted, where we receive in our hands the tokens of his love and of his passion in the bread and the wine. Again and again I have found that, when I have slipped, there are the hands of God waiting to set me on my feet and get me going again: "Keeping us firm", as the prayer says, "in the hope that he sets before us".'

But is there a contradiction between the God who meets you to take you home, and the God who will set you free?

'No, ultimately I don't think there is. Of course, in the parable, we don't know what happened to the prodigal son when the father's arms had opened and taken him back home again. But I think in Christian experience God receives a man or a woman back home, forgives him and reinstates him, not in order that he may just have a nice time and be a pious human being, but that he may go out into the world bringing with him the newness of life which he himself has found.'

Lord Coggan. Archbishop of Canterbury, 1974–80; Archbishop of York, 1961–74.

Father of all,
we give you thanks and praise,
that when we were still far off
you met us in your Son and brought us home.
Dying and living,
he declared your love,
gave us grace,
and opened the gate of glory.
May we who share Christ's body live his risen life;
we who drink his cup bring life to others;
we whom the Spirit lights give light to the world.
Keep us firm in the hope you have set before us,
so we and all your children shall be free,
and the whole earth live to praise your name;
through Christ our Lord.

Professor David Frost
The Alternative Service Book 1980

31

Felicitas Corrigan

'From childhood I have realized that there are only two people in the whole world that really mattered. God and me.'

A lifetime later, it is the most simple of poems which expresses the relationship between her and God. The lines were composed by one of the other sisters of the Benedictine Abbey at Stanbrook, where Dame Felicitas has spent almost six decades in devotion and prayer. I describe them as a poem of love between the individual and God, and I ask what makes this love so different from any other love.

'We are talking about the love of revelation and the God of revelation. We have in our human experience a faint adumbration of a reality that is immense and mysterious, and completely beyond any experience of our own as a human being. And that is what we mean by love. And when God loves me, he has expressed that love. We have only got to look at a crucifix and we see how God's love has expressed itself in his own son, torn to pieces on a gibbet. That is what love does. It is crucified.'

But to go further and say that 'God loves me as he loves nobody else' seems to contradict the essence of universal love. Are the same elements of his love not available to all people?

'The same elements are available to all people, but all people do not avail themselves of those elements. And the whole point is, as I said to begin with, that there are only two people in the whole world who matter, God and me. I am not responsible for my neighbour. I am not responsible for the fact that I came into the world. But here I am, and I know that I am a personality that will have to answer responsibly to the God who made me. I do not know how my neighbour reacts to God's love, that is known only to God. The psalmist tells us that God made hearts one by one. If you look at the hundreds of millions of different faces in the world, no two faces are alike. The artist has not made only faces but souls and hearts. What do we mean by heart? We are talking about some secret place that is known only to God and to you.'

Does your love of God depend upon his love for you?

'My love of God depends upon my acceptance of his will in every department of my life. Even though it seems terribly hard to accept, his sacrificial love will make me realize that no matter how life is treating me, God's wisdom is much greater than mine and that his will is to be accepted as his divine will for me. "Not my will, but thine be done." There is love.'

Felicitas Corrigan. Nun of Stanbrook Abbey, since 1933. Author: Siegfried Sassoon: Poet's Pilgrimage (1973); Songs of the Wandering Scholars (1982); Helen Waddell: a biography (1986); Editor: Between Two Eternities: A Helen Waddell Anthology (1993).

God loves me
as nobody else loves me
and as he loves nobody else.

I love God
as nobody else loves him
and as I love nobody else.

written by a nun of Stanbrook Abbey

Caroline Cox

'In my prayer life, I try to get a balance between myself talking to God, and being still and available for him to talk to me or relate to me in whatever way he chooses.'

Baroness Cox's inspiration comes from part of a poem by the American Quaker John Greenleaf Whittier. One verse in particular is filled with his conviction that it is in stillness not excitement that God is found. His intriguing imagery of the 'dropping dews' raises thoughts of an inevitable, perhaps cyclic, presence of God.

'I think there is a cycle, but what is so glorious about God's grace is that it is available at any time. I try to be available to God in a regular way in my prayer time, and I think it is wonderful that by using a prayer like this, even in the middle of the hustle and bustle of a busy day, one can feel grace and quietness.'

Is this enough to do away with strain and stresses?

'By removing strain and stress, one is not going to go into a life of apathy and laziness. It is a question about one's own striving, putting that into the context of what God is trying to do for your own life, and striving on behalf of what God is asking of us. It is not about contriving for oneself, but about being open to God's guidance and putting oneself into his hands to use us (me in this case) as he would want to. Therefore it is less of my contriving and striving and more of my being available to serve him. I think the strain and stress of life can be alleviated by praying this kind of prayer, and hoping that he will use it for his purposes, while at the same time trying in one's life to be open to his spirit. After all, the fruits of the spirit are love, joy and peace, and I think those can be experienced even through activity, and even through strain and stress.

'There have been times when I have seen the beauty of God's peace. I have found that when I have taken time out as systematically as I can, and made time for worship through still and silent adoration, I have felt the presence of God very deeply and very powerfully, and in a way that is very strengthening and very peaceful.'

Baroness Cox. A Deputy Speaker, House of Lords, since 1986. Director, Nursing Education Research Unit, Chelsea College, University of London, 1977–84.

34

Drop thy still dews of quietness,
Till all our strivings cease;
Take from our souls the strain and stress,
And let our ordered lives confess
The beauty of thy peace.

from 'The Brewing of Soma'
John Greenleaf Whittier (1807–92)
(sung as the hymn 'Dear Lord and Father of Mankind')

Don Cupitt

Here is a bringing together of old and new. A controversial Cambridge theologian chooses the ancient prayer which became the Collect for Purity in Cranmer's 1549 Order of Holy Communion.

Its invocation to an omniscient God provides meat for discussion.

'One meaning of the word "God" is that God functions as a standard of perfection by which we can hold our own lives. So for me the prayer functions to call us to recollection and to concentration, and to an inner clarity of mind. The word "spirit" implies consciousness, so that God's spirit is something like God's consciousness. I think we should not think of God as a separate being outside the world. In an age of science, we don't need the idea of God in that sense. But we do need the idea of God as a symbol, a spiritual ideal of perfection and a standard of integrity and purity.

'The traditional idea of God as omniscient, knowing everything, is sometimes taken to imply that God is a sort of super-computer in whose data banks everything is stored. That is not really the meaning of the idea. The idea is simply that God is a standard before which you cannot hide anything and should not conceal the truth from yourself. Human beings are very prone to self-deception, and the prayer is a challenge to that.'

The prayer asks for cleansing and the perfection of love.

'For me "cleansing" means "clarity", or concentration or elimination of distractions. I think that is all it is. I don't think it means repression or the forbidding of thoughts.'

How is your love of God 'imperfect'?

'I think of the love of God as a sort of objectless love. Most human love is very selective. We choose this and we reject that. We love one thing and we hate another. The love of God, I think, means a universal and objectless love of all creation for all things. I don't think of the love of God as being fixated on a separate being who happens to be extra big and outside the world. I think that is too crude and primitive a notion.'

How would you expect to be able to magnify his name worthily?

'By living like Christ does. All Christian prayer is to God through Christ, because he gives us that redefinition of the idea of God.'

Revd Don Cupitt. Dean of Emmanuel College, Cambridge, since 1965, and Lecturer in Divinity, University of Cambridge, since 1973.

Almighty God,
unto whom all hearts be open,
all desires known,
and from whom no secrets are hid:
Cleanse the thoughts of our hearts
by the inspiration of thy Holy Spirit,
that we may perfectly love thee,
and worthily magnify thy holy Name;
through Christ our Lord.

attributed to St Gregory, Abbot of Canterbury *c*.780
The Book of Common Prayer (1662)

Cahal Daly

'I find it an extremely helpful prayer in times of indecision when faced with an important but difficult choice.'

Thomas Merton's prayer is made without petition or plea to God. Its deep simplicity reflects the experience of the Trappist monk from Kentucky who could say with confidence 'I have no idea where I am going'. I put that phrase to Cahal Daly. Does he ever resent the uncertainty of what lies ahead?

'No. I think one should not, because it is part of one's creatureliness. And I think it is right that the prayer should be more concerned about God than about me. Prayer is about God, about my position before God, and about my dependence on God. It means simply letting God be.'

Merton expresses a view of the balance between motive and action: 'I believe that the desire to please you does, in fact, please you'. Is that the bishop's view?

'I am concerned both with what I do and why I do it, because I know very well that you cannot turn a wrong choice into a right one simply by a good motive. But if I am really desiring to do God's will, then I am really hoping and trusting that the thing I do, not just the motive with which I do it, is pleasing to him. But I cannot be sure. I leave it for him to decide. And I firmly believe in trust and in hope, and if that is my attitude, God will accept the thing as done in love and he who is love will understand and will accept something that is done for love and for his glory.

'For me, all confidence comes from the fact that God is God. Very often I want to play God, about my own choices, goodness or sincerity, but the point is to de-centre myself, to find my centre in God and to concentrate on him. Let God be God.'

Cardinal Cahal Daly. Archbishop of Armagh (RC) and Primate of All Ireland, since 1992. Bishop of Down and Connor, 1982–1992.

My Lord God, I have no idea where I am going.
I do not see the road ahead of me.
I cannot know for certain where it will end.
Nor do I really know myself,
and the fact that I think I am following your will
does not mean that I am actually doing so.

But I believe that the desire to please you does in fact please you,
and I hope that I have that desire in all that I am doing.
I hope that I never do anything apart from that desire.
And I know that if I do this
you will lead me by the right road
though I may know nothing about it.

Therefore I will trust you always.
Though I may seem to be lost and in the shadow of death
I will not fear, for you are ever with me
and you will never leave me to face my peril alone.

Thomas Merton (1915–68)

Judi Dench

'When we pray, we surely pray for the lessening of the arduousness of life.'

Perched on a cushion on the floor of her London home, Dame Judi adopts the style of a college student, rather than of a celebrated actress who has starred in films, on television and on stage for more than thirty years.

'As a child I was attracted by the picture of an enormous hand which enclosed you and kept you safe.'

The picture she remembers comes from a Gaelic blessing full of comfort and optimism. Its opening words, 'may the road rise to meet you', lead me to wonder whether she has been carried down some unexpected roads.

'I have never found the road I am on is the expected one,' she admits. 'Never! I am one of those people who go through life thinking I know what the next bit will be like, and then get the dangerous bend and go straight into the hedge. But I have a kind of fatalism in me which believes the road you choose probably is the road you have to go on, however hard it is.

'It is rather like trying to work on a performance, when you have in front of you millions of buttons, and you have to choose the few you particularly want in order to make that part right. It is almost a microcosm of what you do in life, stepping forward in an instinctive kind of way.'

If the line 'may the rain fall softly upon your fields' suggests the need for nourishment from God, what provides that nourishment for her?

'I can only think it is the strength which comes from fellow men, perhaps through people's kindness. I suppose that is one of the reasons why Quakerism is such a great comfort for me, the idea that where several people are gathered together, there is a fellowship about that group of people which gives me strength.

'I am not a person who is very good at being on my own, and certainly not when working. Often I have been asked to do something on my own, and I cannot do it. I need tremendously the closeness and the companionship of other people and I suppose that is God through other men. All of us are made in the likeness of God, and that shows through the innate goodness which you can feel from other people.'

Dame Judi Dench. Actress. Films include: A Room with a View; 84 Charing Cross Road; A Handful of Dust. *Television appearances include:* Talking to a Stranger; A Fine Romance; Mr and Mrs Edgehill; As Time Goes By.

May the road rise to meet you,
May the wind be always at your back,
May the sun shine warm upon your face,
May the rains fall softly upon your fields.
Until we meet again,
May God hold you in the hollow of his hand.

Gaelic Blessing

Robin Eames

It is almost impossible to equate the beauty of the seemingly tranquil countryside of County Armagh, and the warmth of the people who live there, with the scenes of brutality, murder and horrific violence which are associated with that place. Arriving early for my appointment I spend a moment or two in the tiny Anglican Cathedral in Armagh, a place, it seems, of solace and peace. But it is the reality of the situation for those who live there which dictates the choice of prayer for the Anglican Archbishop of Armagh.

'In a situation of tremendous violence and tension, with gunfire in their ears and the smell of burning in their nostrils, a group met together for a short service of prayer before the night came on. We weren't certain which prayers to use. Then someone said "there is a prayer that I think is very appropriate because it speaks in terms of light and darkness". Suddenly it dawned on us that it was this very traditional prayer from the Prayer Book which seemed so appropriate as night came on and in that situation when no one knew quite what was going to happen.

'Often, though, I think of "darkness" here as the darkness of uncertainty, violence, prejudice and bigotry. It is the darkness that comes from those who have lost their way, the darkness of suffering and injustice. But chiefly, in the Christian sense, it is the darkness that comes from people who may find that their faith has not only been challenged but has been eroded by the situation in which they live.

'I think the "defence" referred to in this collect is formed very simply on a personal basis, because I am a great believer in a personal faith. My experience has been that very often in the most astonishing circumstances you get wonderful examples of courage and faith which you would least expect. So to me, a light shining in the darkness isn't just an indefinable dogmatic thing, it is the light of a person's own life, their hope and courage. I think "defence" is a misunderstood word, which means different things to different people. It is not that the Christian life is going to be defended from the ills that happen to everyone else. Just the opposite. Christ never promised us a carpet to paradise. He promised us that if we wanted to follow him, we were to take up our cross, deny ourselves and follow him. What did it lead to? It led to Calvary. But Calvary was the stepping stone to the future which was Easter morning. So that is the defensiveness. It is courage, faith and strength. That, I believe, the world desperately needs.'

Most Revd Robin Eames. Archbishop of Armagh (Anglican) and Primate of All Ireland, since 1986. Chairman, Commission on Communion and Women in the Episcopate, since 1988.

Lighten our darkness,
we beseech thee, O Lord;
and by thy great mercy
defend us from all perils
and dangers of this night;
for the love of thy only Son,
our Saviour
Jesus Christ.

Collect for Aid against all Perils
The Book of Common Prayer (1662)

Elizabeth Esteve-Coll

The Director's room at the Victoria and Albert Museum has the most remarkable approach that any office could have. Surrounded by hundreds of thousands of the nation's most priceless treasures, it sits amidst fragments of centuries, lives and beliefs barely known, which stretch back to times long before Christ walked on earth. Who knows what the world might have known while some of the oldest relics were fashioned anew?

The Director has asked to discuss a poem written perhaps a thousand years or more before Christ, but which forms part of the collection which has most influenced Christian worship in the East and the West. Psalm 121 speaks first of dependence upon God and then of his constancy and protection towards mankind.

'I tend to turn to God not only in moments of crisis (of course I do then) but at odd moments during the day. It is contact with people, or things that I see in the street or read about that make me turn to God and consciously ask for help and support. When you are dealing with a difficult question of inter-personal relationships, and you may not have been able to give someone the strength or the comfort they were looking for because you have not been able to draw it out of yourself, you turn to God to ask for assistance in giving what is needed, which is greater than yourself.

'I think very much that God is constant and eternal, and that there is a stable relationship which never changes with mood or politics. That gives me immense comfort. I am aware that you are constantly exposed to evil. For many years I found it difficult to believe that evil existed. But I think as you grow older, you become more and more aware of the manifestations of evil; and, yes, I do believe, with the psalmist, that there is this all-embracing protection. I believe that there is free will to commit evil, but that if you accept the word of the Lord, then there is the possibility of keeping your soul from evil.'

Elizabeth Esteve-Coll. Director, Victoria and Albert Museum, since 1988.

I will lift up mine eyes unto the hills:
from whence cometh my help.

My help cometh even from the Lord:
who hath made heaven and earth.

He will not suffer thy foot to be moved:
and he that keepeth thee will not sleep.

Behold, he that keepeth Israel:
shall neither slumber nor sleep.

The Lord himself is thy keeper:
the Lord is thy defence upon thy right hand;

So that the sun shall not burn thee by day:
neither the moon by night.

The Lord shall preserve thee from all evil:
yea, it is even he that shall keep thy soul.

The Lord shall preserve thy going out, and thy coming in:
from this time forth for evermore.

Psalm 121
The Book of Common Prayer (1662)

Ken Flach

This was my first experience of Wimbledon beyond the tight parameters of the television screen. Just outside the picture lies a world of excited and exciting activity. Broadcasters and journalists scramble for the attention of players who re-live their tense moments of victory and loss. Crowds throng around the players' door, hoping for a glimpse of their favourite stars.

I have come to meet a man who knows victory here. Three times Ken Flach has held the doubles championship cup above his head. But the glamorous touring life, he confesses, has also caused him some difficulties.

'Before I became a Christian, or before I was even married, life on the tennis tour was a life of great temptation. There are many female admirers around the tennis courts. Guys like to go out and party together and go to the bars, and this is my weakest area. For some people it might be alcohol, or it might be drugs, or for some people it might even be food. With me it has been sex. But with God's guidance in my life, and wanting to please him, I am able to do what it says here, in that my wife's breasts alone satisfy me.

'I have been over here in Europe for five of the last six weeks. I was two weeks in Paris, I went home for a week, and have been here for three weeks. So this passage from Proverbs is very pertinent to me. When there are a lot of rain delays and a lot of time off, and being away from my wife for that long, it is something I need to stay close to.

'The Lord coming into my life has helped me a great deal in this regard, because the temptations are still there, but with his strength I am able to resist them. That is why it is so important to come back to Proverbs. And the biggest thing, too, is staying in God's word, remaining in the Bible, reading, getting strength, encouragement and nourishment that I need when I am away by myself, on my own, with a lot of time on my hands.

'What motivates me most is that I am in full view of the Lord. I try sometimes to imagine, especially when I am playing in a match, that Jesus is in the crowd, and, if he were watching me, how I would perform or behave. That really helps me a lot, and if you envisage yourself with Christ then you won't do the things that Satan is tempting you to do. You will realize that it is wrong, and that it is not pleasing to God, and you don't want to sin against him.'

Ken Flach. American tennis player. Winner: (with Seguso) US Open, 1985; Wimbledon, 1987, Wimbledon, 1988; Olympics gold medal, 1988; (with Kathy Jordan) French Open, 1986; Wimbledon, 1986.

Drink water from your own cistern,
running water from your own well.
Should your springs overflow in the streets,
your streams of water in the public squares?
Let them be yours alone,
never to be shared with strangers.
May your fountain be blessed,
and may you rejoice in the wife of your youth.
A loving doe, a graceful deer —
may her breasts satisfy you always,
may you ever be captivated by her love.
Why be captivated, my son, by an adulteress?
Why embrace the bosom of another man's wife?
For a man's ways are in full view of the Lord,
and he examines all his paths.
The evil deeds of a wicked man ensnare him;
the chords of his sin hold him fast.
He will die for lack of discipline,
led astray by his own great folly.

Proverbs 5.15–23
(New International Version)

James Fox

Persecution and conspiracy. The stuff of screenplay drama is seen in the real-life experiences of believers living in the first few years of the Christian Church. Their plight is described by St Luke in a passage from Acts which contains the first recorded prayer of the early church. It is a passage which has provided inspiration to the actor James Fox.

'You see the level of spirituality of the early Christians in it, and how they dealt with overt persecution in their day. The leaders were under sentence of death if they spoke about the gospel, and they felt their lives were at risk. But it teaches us about the God they knew, and can deepen our own understanding of who he is.

'The believers of tho⸜e days looked into the scriptures and they discovered that God had already spoken about the events they had witnessed. So they found explanation, and, drawing comfort from that, found boldness to proclaim the only means by which man can be reconciled. This is where the early Christians can really help us. They were praying within a few months of the crucifixion of Jesus, who they were now calling "Lord", "God" and "King". So we see that the early Church understood God as a "hands-on" God, and a God who even purposed that his son should be rejected by earthly rulers and crucified. We must view our present circumstances in the light of God's dealings with us, in his correcting us and his seeking to get our attention.

'The early believers felt vulnerable and very frightened, and in the face of challenge, I would certainly need, as they did, to recognize afresh who God was, to recognize what he wanted, and to cry out for boldness in prayer. For boldness comes in answer to prayer by the power of the Holy Spirit.'

James Fox. Actor. Left acting from 1970–79 to pursue Christian vocation. Main films include: The Servant, *1963;* King Rat, *1964;* The Chase, *1966;* Performance, *1969;* A Passage to India, *1984;* The Russia House, *1990.*

Sovereign Lord,
you made the heaven and the earth and the sea,
and everything in them.
You spoke by the Holy Spirit
through the mouth of your servant,
our father David:

'Why do the nations rage
and the peoples plot in vain?
The kings of the earth take their stand
and the rulers gather together against the Lord
and against his Anointed One.'

Indeed Herod and Pontius Pilate met together
with the Gentiles and the people of Israel
in this city
to conspire against your holy servant Jesus,
whom you anointed.
They did what your power and will had decided beforehand should
    happen.
Now, Lord,
consider their threats
and enable your servants to speak your word with great boldness.
Stretch out your hand to heal
and perform miraculous signs and wonders
through the name of your holy servant Jesus.

Acts 4.24b–30
(New International Version)

49

John Habgood

'In my own mind the visual imagery underlying this prayer is that of the tide coming in. Standing on the shore, you can imagine the tide, as it comes in, turning dull pebbles into beautiful jewels in the sea, making the seaweed glisten, and bringing back the fish. So the coming of God is intimately associated with seeing the world in a new way and seeing it as God's gift.'

In practice, can you see those gifts identified in the prayer (fourth line onwards) in the tidy way which its list of experiences past, present and future might suggest?

'No, because prayers divide up total experience into words and phrases. I think one can see life in the total context of God's activity. It is an activity which can heal the past, and I think the healing of the past and the calming of memories are very important parts of Christian experience. This is another way of talking about forgiveness and all the possibilities of new life and joy which flow out of that.'

How do you ensure that what you do is drawn from God?

'You don't, because you cannot separate out what belongs to you and what belongs to God. In relation to love, for example, the fact is that we love because we were first loved. And in love, giving and receiving are two parts of the same activity. It is the same in learning to live in God's strength. In the first instance, you need to know and come to terms with your own weakness and in doing that you find a new strength to live.'

There is an important difference between the first and the last lines: to the same plea 'give us yourself', the last line adds 'help us to give ourselves to you'. What does the Archbishop give to God?

'Let me go back to the original image of standing on the seashore and watching the tide come in. The twist at the end is that the tide coming in is not simply something that you watch, but something into which you plunge. And it is in God's coming that we are enabled to let ourselves go, into the ocean of God's presence and his love.'

Most Revd and Rt Hon. John Habgood. Archbishop of York, since 1983; Bishop of Durham, 1973–83.

O Lord, give us yourself above all things.
It is in your coming alone that we are enriched.
It is in your coming that your true gifts come.
Come, Lord, that we may share the gifts of your Presence.
Come, Lord, with healing of the past,
Come and calm our memories,
Come with joy for the present,
Come and give life to our existence,
Come with hope for the future,
Come and give a sense of eternity.
Come with strength for our wills,
Come with power for our thoughts,
Come with love for our heart,
Come and give affection to our being.
Come, Lord, give yourself above all things
And help us to give ourselves to you.

'O Lord, Give Us'
David Adam (b. 1936)
(from *Tides and Seasons*, SPCK/Triangle 1989)

Lord Hailsham

'People always think of prayers in terms of asking for things, but that is not what prayer is. It is the conscious turning of the soul towards God, like the flower turns to the sun for its light, or the child turns to its mother for comfort and love. It is a natural movement of the soul in adoration.'

Worshippers have long turned to God in the words of the Gloria as they prepare themselves to receive the holy sacrament. But a curious note in one fourth-century Syrian tract, in which maidens are advised to say every morning 'Glory to God in the highest, and the rest' hints at one danger of these venerated and familiar texts. Can an expression of praise become routine?

'Oh yes. In repetition there is always a danger, even in the Lord's Prayer, of repeating it mechanically. But one must try not to. It ought to be a genuine expression in words of exultation of what you feel towards the infinite deity. It exclaims in words, almost of ecstasy, the longing one has for union with God, and one finds ordinary language and ordinary power of composition is not enough.'

The central petition of the prayer is dressed in several different ways. But it is the same petition for mercy against the sins of the world. Is there not an almost obsessive tone underlying this prayer?

'A lot of people would suppose that was true. People say we should not "bewail our sins and wickednesses", as the General Confession has it. I often get letters from people who think that all you have got to do is to have this act of faith which is constantly referred to in the Pauline letters, and then go away whistling a merry tune. But one has constantly to recognize one's fallen nature and constantly to ask for forgiveness, and I think this is very much in accordance with the Lord's Prayer as well.

'You will find, in the Old Testament, Isaiah saying, "pray without ceasing", and I think that is about it. Your ultimate destination is to desire unity with God, and when you have achieved that, you have achieved everything. And unless you have achieved that, you have achieved nothing.'

Lord Hailsham. Lord High Chancellor of Great Britain, 1970–74 and 1979–87. First Lord of the Admiralty, 1956–7. Minister for Science and Technology, 1959–64.

Glory be to God on high,
and in earth peace,
good will towards men.
We praise thee,
we bless thee,
we worship thee,
we glorify thee,
we give thanks to thee for thy great glory,
O Lord God, heavenly King,
God the Father Almighty.

O Lord,
the only-begotten Son, Jesus Christ;
O Lord God,
Lamb of God,
Son of the Father,
that takest away the sins of the world,
have mercy upon us.
Thou that takest away the sins of the world,
have mercy upon us.
Thou that takest away the sins of the world,
receive our prayer.
Thou that sittest at the right hand of God the Father,
have mercy upon us.

For thou only art holy;
thou only art the Lord;
thou only, O Christ,
with the Holy Ghost,
art most high
in the glory of God the Father.

The Book of Common Prayer (1662)

Denis Healey

'I think this poem by R. S. Thomas throws light on many of the problems that worry particularly modern people who cannot understand how you reconcile God with the existence of evil, which is perhaps more apparent in the world today than it has been for centuries.'

R. S. Thomas was born a few years before Denis Healey. The Welsh parson won the Queen's Medal for Poetry in the year Denis Healey became a cabinet minister in the Wilson Government. The Cholmondeley Award came in the year Lord Healey became Chancellor of the Exchequer. The politician freely acknowledges his debt to the work of poets in his understanding of God.

The first part of Thomas's poem struggles with a perception of God, by naming the creator in terms of what is created. Is he also caught up in that conundrum of perception?

'It doesn't worry me so much myself because I haven't ever had much time for theology, and I think to try to systematize the spirit is to deform and destroy it. Thomas points out that men have believed in God right through history, but have seen God in various ways: sometimes as a representation of the impulses in themselves, and sometimes as a representation of the forces in nature, like thunder. And it is only really since the Christian era that people have seen God as love.'

What's your own perception of God?

'Very much the latter, but then I don't like to try to define it in words, because I think that is inevitably to malform it. The philosopher I most like, and who gave me more knowledge of the world than anybody else, was Immanuel Kant, who destroyed knowledge to make room for belief. This is something which the poor theologians never understand.

'I think the unique thing about the Christian religion is the idea that God sent his own son to earth to suffer with men, to pardon them and to redeem them, and Christians have worried about this symbol right through history, and are still worrying, but it is a very powerful symbol which relates a tortured body, nailed to a cross, to the concept of an all-embracing love.'

Lord Healey. Chancellor of the Exchequer, 1974–79; Secretary of State for Defence, 1964–70, and member of the Shadow Cabinet 1959–64, 1970–4, 1979–87. Served in the Second World War, attaining rank of Major.

Tell Us

We have had names for you:
The Thunderer, the Almighty
Hunter, Lord of the snowflake
and the sabre-toothed tiger.
One name we have held back
unable to reconcile it
with the mosquito, the tidal-wave,
the black hole into which
time will fall. You have answered
us with the image of yourself
on a hewn tree, suffering
injustice, pardoning it;
pointing as though in either
direction; horrifying us
with the possibility of dislocation.
Ah, love, with your arms out
wide, tell us how much more
they must still be stretched
to embrace a universe drawing
away from us at the speed of light.

R. S. Thomas (b. 1913)
from *Mass for Hard Times* (Bloodaxe Books, 1992)

John Hermon

Looking out from the upstairs window of his house, I cannot ignore the angry juxtaposition which stares at me. The beautiful panorama of the Irish coast stretches away for miles. But outside his home, just below, a security guard keeps his watch. Even in retirement, Sir John cannot completely leave behind the evil men he has encountered during the years as Chief Constable of the Royal Ulster Constabulary. So what does he make of a prayer which knows God as 'creator and preserver of all mankind'?

'I think we tend sometimes to look simplistically towards God to correct all our weaknesses and restore the consequences of our wrong. My view is that this prayer reflects God's will and our request to God to be given this type of will. But we must not forget that God looks to his people to perform his miracles, and live in a way which is conducive to those standards he sets us. Any faults there are in our world today cannot be placed at the door of God, but rather at the door of the people who populate this world, and possibly those leaders within the world who should be leading in different and better directions.

'God is God, and he is everlasting. I have no belief in the sanctity of life for individuals, because the evidence of that in places of starvation, deprivation and disease shows that there is no sanctity for so many people who are equal in the eyes of God. My clear belief is that it is the people who are more favoured, more blessed, or more fortunate because of the area in which they live or the circumstances of their living who should be doing more for the underprivileged to even this out. That is God's will.

'The reality is that we are here, and have come so far. It is a very early stage in our evolution, although we tend to think otherwise because of the sophistication of our knowledge. The wonder to me, after the trauma of mistakes which tribes and nations have made over the centuries, is that we exist at all. The fact that we do, and that God's word is prevalent throughout the world in so many places, is grounds for a very solid hope for the future. I believe this prayer says to the people: you must perform God's will; it is you who occupy this planet and in God's name you will improve the standard of it for those people who are living in it, and for those people who will follow you. That, I believe, is God's will.'

Sir John Hermon. Chief Constable, Royal Ulster Constabulary, 1980–89.

O God,
creator and preserver of all mankind;
bless the people of all nations,
reconcile those who are divided,
relieve the hungry and oppressed,
bring joy to the sorrowing,
and peace and hope to all;
through Jesus Christ, our Lord.

The Alternative Prayer Book 1984
(Church of Ireland)

Thora Hird

'I think this could have been written today, you know. It was written by a seventeenth-century nun, but it is very modern writing and there is so much of this that any of us my age could say, and mean very sincerely.'

It had taken us quite some time to get to the studio. Several old friends spotted Thora as we made our way down, and, even in that short journey, she made a few new friends on the way. Now, as we sit talking across the green felt-topped table, even the gloomy basement studio takes on a remarkably homely feel.

'I know what that line means', she says. ' "Make me thoughtful but not moody, helpful but not bossy" means, do stop me clever-heading with everybody and knowing better than they do how to do anything. It does happen more with elder people, and don't forget that I am talking now as someone who has grown old, and I know these things that you are inclined to do. Someone is doing a job, and you are inclined to chuck your little bit in, saying, "Oh, and now you will have to do so and so . . ." and they *know* what they will have to do.

'And "Seal my lips on my aches and pains" means, do stop me nattering about it.'

For a moment her face twists in a shooting pain. She moans in convincing agony.

'Even if it's only that', she says, the twinkly smile returning to her face.

'I have got arthritis, and I have got it pretty badly, but I have got a couple of replacement hips which have eased it a little. But now I have got it at the base of my spine, and they can't give me a new spine. But I say to myself, how dare I say how painful my legs are? There are some people without legs! It doesn't make me any better than anybody else, but it makes me shut up a bit.

'And that's another thing: "Give me the ability to see good things in unexpected places and talents in unexpected people." We all meet people who you look at and think, nobody has ever said to you how nice you look, nobody has ever said to you "Aren't you a nice writer" or "You look nice in blue". And it is so easy. I don't think there is anybody walking about whom, if you just give it a tick or two, you couldn't say something: "You have got beautiful teeth, excuse me being so personal", that sort of thing. I bet I read this prayer twenty times before it really struck me what everything meant, but this is how I look at it because these words are so simple.'

Dame Thora Hird. Actress. Television programmes include: Meet the Wife; Hallelujah!; Last of the Summer Wine; Flesh and Blood; Praise Be!

Lord,
Thou knowest better than I know myself,
that I am growing older and will some day be old.
Keep me from the fatal habit of thinking I must say something
on every subject and on every occasion.
Release me from craving to straighten out everybody's affairs.
Make me thoughtful but not moody;
helpful but not bossy.
With my vast store of wisdom, it seems a pity not to use it all,
but Thou knowest, Lord,
that I want a few friends at the end.

Keep my mind free from the recital of endless details;
give me the wings to get to the point.
Seal my lips on my aches and pains.
They are increasing,
and love of rehearsing them is becoming sweeter as the years go by.
I dare not ask for grace enough to enjoy the tales of others' pains,
but help me to endure them with patience.

I dare not ask for improved memory,
but for a growing humility,
and a lessening cocksureness
when my memory seems to clash with the memory of others.
Teach me the glorious lesson that occasionally I may be mistaken.
Keep me reasonably sweet.
I do not want to be a saint
(some of them are so hard to live with)
but a sour old person is one of the crowning works of the devil.
Give me the ability to see good things in unexpected places
and talents in unexpected people.
And give me, O Lord,
the grace to tell them so.

A seventeenth-century nun

Richard Holloway

'This is a companion's prayer. It calls for courage, it reminds us that the life of faith is not predictable, and may involve uncertainty, pain and suffering. But underpinning it, as there is underpinning the life of faith even in the midst of the most tragic circumstances, there is a sense of being companioned by God, who, while God may not remove the sorrow, is an arm around the shoulder, helping us to bear it.'

I am struck by something unusual: the petitions of the prayer are never made directly to God. For a companion's prayer, isn't this a timid way to pray?

'I don't know why Bede Jarrett wrote it like this. He was a man of immense spiritual depth and a man who had also suffered, and it is conceivable that this prayer was formed in a particular context that I don't know about. But I do not like to address God like some sort of sleepy donkey who really ought to wake up. I think God is mystery – loving mystery – and I think that this prayer reflects that sense of God as being a profound and depthless mystery, with whom we can have communion, but whom we cannot exactly comprehend.'

That relationship is intriguing in the context of what follows: 'if he bids us climb a hill, may we not notice it's a hill, mindful only of the happiness of his company'. Isn't there a hint that the relationship is so close that you fail to see things around you as they are?

'Yes. I am a hill walker and that is another reason why I like this prayer. If you are walking up a hill in deep conversation with a friend, you don't notice that it is a hill. Obviously you cannot have a profound conversation if you are scrambling up a rock face, but if you are going up a reasonably steep hill, talking animatedly to a friend, you get to the top, and you suddenly realize that you have gone up quite a steep ascent. It is in that sense that he is meaning it: that if we are so companioned by God, we will not notice that life's difficulties are as difficult as other people think they are.'

What are the unveiled beauties you want to see by travelling with God?

'I want to know in what forms the veils of this life come. We do not know God in the fullness of divinity. We long for that revelation, but we do not yet have it. One day we will know as we are presently known. This is quite an erotic prayer in a way, almost the prayer of a lover wanting to see his beloved unveiled. It is a prayer of longing for that consummation, when all veils will be ripped off, and we will be face to face with our beloved.'

Rt Revd Richard Holloway. Bishop of Edinburgh, since 1986.

May he give us
   all the courage that we need
      to go the way he shepherds us.

That when he calls
   we may go unfrightened.

If he bids us come to him
   across the waters,
      that unfrightened we may go.

And if he bids us climb a hill,
   may we not notice that it is a hill,
      mindful only of
         the happiness of his company.

He made us for himself,
   that we should travel with him
      and see him at the last
         in his unveiled beauty
      in the abiding city where
      he is light
         and happiness
         and endless home.

Bede Jarrett (1881–1934)
(Dominican priest and Prior of Blackfriars, Oxford)

David Hope

AD 314. Barely three hundred years after Jesus walked on earth a Bishop of London is named at the Council of Arles. The see of London was officially established later, in 604, but it is awesome to imagine such a line of continuous ministry active in the capital city of England stretching back so near to the time of Christ.

On the eve of his enthronement as the one-hundred-and-thirty-first Bishop of London, David Hope is about to take on one of the most difficult English dioceses and steer it through another era of Christian witness. His thoughts are on the words of a timeless prayer, used and repeated by generations of faithful in the orthodox tradition.

It is a prayer which reflects his belief that God is present at all times, and in all places. Will he, then, trace every happening in life directly back to God?

'Very often I begin to think, "Is God in all this?", or "Is this really God's will?" Particularly with difficulties and painful events I begin to see, in time, that there is something creative about even the worst things, even if I cannot agree that God has directly caused a thing to happen.'

Later in the prayer there is a call for strength to bear the fatigue of the coming day. Does that tie up with the original supplication of the prayer for peace?

'I don't know about you, but I find if I begin to get tired I get very irritable and a bit tetchy. Once I begin to be irritable, then people around me get irritable, and it sets up a whole kind of reverberation of lack of peace and stability. So I do pray that, when I get tired, the Lord will actually support and sustain me, and give me the good sense to put my feet up and relax a bit, and then I will be refreshed and renewed in order to face things again in a rather more positive way.'

The prayer ends with those same words which end the prayer chosen by Metropolitan Anthony: 'Pray thou thyself in me'. In seeking that relationship with God, is it not possible to lose sight of the individual?

'No, because I believe that God's will is that I should be the person he has created me to be. It is me who so often gets in the way, and my fallen nature which wants to carry me off in directions other than that he would will for me. God does take me, and every other person, very seriously. Each individual is created in the divine image and it is in order to enable me to be more me, that I have to allow the spirit of the living God to pray in me.'

Rt Revd David Hope. Bishop of London since 1992; Bishop of Wakefield 1985–92.

O Lord,
Grant me to greet the coming day in peace.
Help me in all things to rely upon thy holy will.
In every hour of the day reveal thy will to me.
Bless my dealings with all who surround me.
Teach me to treat all that comes to me throughout the day
with peace of soul
and with firm conviction
that thy will governs all.
In all my deeds and words,
guide my thoughts and feelings.
In unforeseen events let me not forget that all are sent by thee.
Teach me to act firmly and wisely
without embittering and embarrassing others.
Give me strength to bear the fatigue of the coming day
with all that it shall bring.
Direct my will.
Teach me to pray.
Pray thou thyself in me.

Russian Orthodox prayer

Susan Howatch

'Back in 1987 I was going through a very bad time. I had to move house for the third time in two years, and my personal life was very wrecked. I thought, "No, I can't go on, I don't know what to do." So I thought I would go to hear the new Dean of Guildford (Alex Wedderspoon) preach. I went out of that cathedral thinking I could conquer the world, it so totally turned me around.'

The text which the Dean of Guildford used came from the letter of Paul to the Romans. Its transforming power came from the new light shed on the phrase 'all things *work together* for good to them that love God'.

'The Dean pointed out that it should be translated, "God *intermingles* all things for good for those who love him". There is an intermingling. Life is a mixture of despair and hope, and no matter how dark it is, there is always the light shining beyond it. It is the interplay of the light on the dark that gives meaning to life, and if you can see the meaning in the suffering, then it becomes easier to endure. So I would say that this verse enables me to face the really bad things of life, and try to find meaning in them, knowing all the time that beyond is the divine purpose or providence. One must have faith that there is meaning, and then even the most dreadful experiences can be endured.'

But if *all* things intermingle for good, is there a place even for evil in the lives of those who strive to do good?

'That would be a twisting of the quotation, and the most facile reading. Of course you often find people who say suffering is good for you, and they are always the people who live comfortably with three meals a day and a nice income. The point of the quotation is not to deny suffering, but to accept it, and to see that God is always working to redeem the suffering.

'The verse also interests me because it is about God the creator. I am certainly not God, but I *am* in the business of creation, and I know that creation is a very difficult and painstaking process. You make a lot of errors, but always you are slaving to make everything come right. So no matter what ghastly things go wrong in this world you have created for yourself, you are always trying to redeem it, bringing truth out of falsehood and reality out of illusion. I think that would be the underlying negation of what you are suggesting. It is not an optimistic view, saying, "Everything is going to be all right in the end, all coming up moonlight and roses." What this approach does is to face the evil and think of God trying to redeem it, and redeem suffering by bringing good out of evil.'

Susan Howatch. Best-selling author. Penmarric; Cashelmara; The Rich Are Different; Sins of the Fathers; The Wheel of Fortune; Glittering Images; Glamorous Powers; Ultimate Prizes; Scandalous Risks; Mystical Paths.

We know that

all things work together for good
to them that love God,

to them who are the called
according to his purpose.

Romans 8.28
(Authorized Version)

Trevor Huddleston

The words of the prophet Isaiah, which once inspired St Paul, now grip Archbishop Huddleston, long-time champion of the anti-apartheid cause. The words formed the invocation of one of the ancient Latin collects, translated in The Book of Common Prayer: 'O God, who hast prepared for them that love thee such good things as pass man's understanding'.

'I find an extraordinary affinity between what we are supposed to understand by the love of and for God, and the love of friendship. As one gets older, one is aware that one's friends are no longer in this world but in the next. I find myself praying just as easily for people who have died as I do for people who are living. And I suppose, subconsciously, or perhaps now consciously, I really look forward to seeing them all again. So I think that the love of friendship is an expression of the love of God in a way that is available to everybody.

'Everything changes as the years progress. One believes more and more in less and less, and holds on to the very basic fundamentals. One is content that God and his love are deeply mysterious, and the attempts that one has made to explain the love of God don't really mean anything, because it is a mystery. So I am content not to know the things that pass my knowledge. I am very content to believe that there will be a fulfilment of all that has been the very best in life, and I count friendship amongst those things, in an absolute and infinite degree.'

Looking simply at the supplication of the prayer, for sufficient love to obtain God's promises, I wonder whether self-interest can properly motivate love.

'I think there is always self-interest in love. We are taught to love our neighbours as ourselves. We are not taught to love our neighbours in abstract. And I think that a right self-interest is not selfishness. The meaning of the prayer for me has always been that it puts into a very concise form something that is virtually inexpressible, namely, the whole motivation and purpose of human existence which is the love of God. In the end it comes down simply to that. There is the unfinished business of life which is going to be completed and fulfilled in glory. And the glory will be the glory of being within the love and presence of God.'

Most Revd Trevor Huddleston. Chairman, International Defence and Aid Fund for Southern Africa, since 1983; Bishop of Masasi 1960–68; Bishop of Stepney 1968–78; Bishop of Mauritius, and Archbishop of the Indian Ocean, 1978–83; President, Anti-Apartheid Movement, since 1981.

O God,
who hast prepared for them that love thee
such good things as pass man's understanding:

Pour into our hearts
such love toward thee,
that we, loving thee above all things,
may obtain thy promises,
which exceed all that we can desire;

through Jesus Christ our Lord.

Collect for the Sixth Sunday after Trinity
(based on 1 Corinthians 2.9 (Isaiah 64.4))
The Book of Common Prayer (1662)

Deus qui diligentibus te bona invisibilia
praeparasti: infunde cordibus nostris tui
amoris affectum ut te in omnibus et super omnia
diligentes promissiones tuas quae omne
desiderium superant consequamur per Dominum.

Gelasian Sacramentary

Basil Hume

'It is a prayer for beginners and a prayer for those who have spent many years trying to pray.'

The choice of an Old Testament text to celebrate an Easter festival speaks deeply of the significance of psalmody in a life of prayer. For a broadcast on the Saturday before Easter, the Cardinal Archbishop of Westminster chooses part of Psalm 63:

'It has a very special significance at Easter because it forms part of the official prayer of the Church, which men and women throughout the world recite on Easter Day. There is a great expression of longing, and of thirsting for God, and, as I pray it, I shall be remembering that other psalm Christ quoted as he was dying on the cross, when he said "my God, my God, why hast thou forsaken me", that terrible cry of anguish as he experienced abandonment and dereliction.

'One of the wonderful things about the psalms is that they not only *express* what we feel and want deep down, but also they help to *form* our feeling and our wanting. This psalm can also be prayed by those who have not been paying a great deal of attention to God in their lives and yet come to him and want to learn something about him. This could be a very appropriate prayer for them to say: "O God, you are my God, for you I long, for you my soul is thirsting", not quite certain what they are longing and thirsting for, but knowing that they are looking for something which will give meaning and purpose to their lives.

'I see a thirsting for God rather, I imagine, as a person who is deeply in love and is not in the company of the beloved, and who pines and longs to be with the person loved. The experience of prayer is that we long to be with God and there is a kind of pining to be with him, to see him as he is and to be united with him. In this present life, that thirst will never be fully quenched. We shall go on thirsting. It can only be fully satisfied when we are united with God, when we are in his sanctuary, when we see his strength and glory. And that glory is to know his love, and to know his beauty.'

Cardinal Basil Hume. Archbishop of Westminster since 1976; Abbot of Ample-forth, 1963–76.

O God,
You are my God,
for you I long,
for you my soul is thirsting.

My body pines for you
like a dry weary land without water.

So I gaze on you in the sanctuary
to see your strength
and your glory.

from Psalm 63

Douglas Hurd

Britain is at war. The liberation of Kuwait has finally begun, with the Allied forces now ending their diplomatic quest to beat Saddam Hussein. Arriving at the Foreign Office just days after the outset of war, when all seems overshadowed by destruction and death, my task is to discover why the British Foreign Secretary, in his only press interview of the day, has asked to discuss the General Thanksgiving, a prayer of thanks for creation and preservation, goodness and loving kindness.

'I think it is always better to begin with thanks. Of course, you go on to pray for all sorts and conditions in man, and particularly for people in distress, but you ought to start with thanks, because, however great the unhappiness, anxieties and sufferings, all of us are surrounded in one way or another by things for which we ought to be thankful. That does not happen by accident, or because we worked hard, it happens because there is a creation and a creator, and, as the prayer goes on, a redeemer. Those are truths which are basic to all the happiness which we have, which is open to us even when there is a lot of anxiety and suffering.

'It is not just the happiness we think of: children, or having a pleasant home, an interesting job, or whatever the different kinds of happiness that people do have. All this is lit up by the facts of religion, which involve faith and the hope of glory. That is the hope that, beyond the satisfaction that you can get in this life, there is a hope of becoming something different through grace, and this is very difficult to grasp at, because it is the mystery of it all. But it is quite right to put it in. It is the climax.'

How is the transition made to show forth his praise not only with our lips, but in our lives?

'That is the key to behaviour. The first bit is the key to belief, and this is the key to behaviour. You have thanked God, but you don't just leave it there, you then have to do something about it, and that is very difficult. It is difficult to change one's feeling of thanksgiving into the extra bit of hard work you do, or the extra bit of thought you give to somebody else, and at times of great pressure, it is even harder than at normal times, when you have more time to reflect on what you might do. But that is what we have to try and do, and that is what we need help in doing.'

Rt Hon. Douglas Hurd. Conservative MP for Witney, since 1983 (Mid-Oxon, 1974–83); Secretary of State for Foreign and Commonwealth Affairs, since 1989; Secretary of State for Northern Ireland, 1984–5; Secretary of State for Home Department, 1985–9.

Almighty God,
Father of all mercies,
we thine unworthy servants do give thee most humble and
  hearty thanks
for all thy goodness and loving-kindness
to us and to all men;

We bless thee for our creation, preservation, and all the blessings
  of this life;
but above all for thine inestimable love
in the redemption of the world by our Lord Jesus Christ,
for the means of grace,
and for the hope of glory.

And we beseech thee, give us that due sense of all thy mercies,
that our hearts may be unfeignedly thankful,
and that we shew forth thy praise,
not only with our lips, but in our lives;
by giving up ourselves to thy service,
and by walking before thee in holiness and righteousness all
  our days;

through Jesus Christ our Lord,
to whom with thee and the Holy Ghost be all honour and glory,
world without end.

Bishop Reynolds (1599–1676)
The Book of Common Prayer (1662)

Richard Ingrams

'I like all of Johnson's prayers, partly because he is always looking into his own failure and inadequacy. He prefaces his prayers with a meditation on his failings over the past year. He always made these annual examinations of his conscience, and I think it is very comforting to find a man of his great achievement and eminence engaged in these acts of great humility.'

This was not the usual fare to come from the writers of *Private Eye*. But as we sit in the offices of the famous satirical magazine, amidst an industry of parody and wit, Richard Ingrams is content, this time, to deliver his words at face value. The same was true of Samuel Johnson when he recorded his diary entries. Away from life at the centre of London's literary circle, he could write with intimate sincerity and self-examination; and no one could be harsher on his own achievement. Johnson looks back at a 'barren waste of time'. He sees 'very little reform' in his practical life. So does Richard Ingrams ever share that feeling which seems so close to despair?

'Not a total despair. But I do have a feeling, more vividly as I get older, of having frittered away my time and not having done anything properly. That is a feeling that I have about my own life and I think it is a feeling that an awful lot of people have. If you look round, it seems an almost obvious observation that people do make terrible messes of their lives, and they do waste their lives and opportunities. And I think that one is constantly making all kinds of resolutions, not just religious resolutions, but books one is going to write, things or travel one is going to do, and when you look back at it you find that, in fact, you have not done any of these things. I am talking from personal experience, but I think it is due to a terrible sloth which afflicts not only me. It is something that all writers are aware of, partly because you sit alone at your desk a lot of the time. It is very easy to get into a day-dreaming state of mind. At the end of the morning you can discover that you have actually done nothing at all.'

So is it realistic to hope that prayer for new resolve will bear fruit?

'I think you have to think that. I think you have to believe that something may result from prayer, otherwise you would not engage in it. And perhaps the most fruitful thing you can do in the form of prayer is not to ask for anything except an awareness of your own faults.'

Richard Ingrams. Editor, Private Eye, *1963–86; Editor,* The Oldie, *since 1992.*

When I survey my past life, I discover nothing but a barren waste of time with some disorders of body and disturbances of the mind very near to madness; which I hope he that made me, will suffer to extenuate many faults, and excuse many deficiencies. Yet much remains to be repented and reformed. I hope that I refer more to God than in former times, and consider more what submission is due to his dispensations. But I have very little reformed my practical life, and the time in which I can struggle with habits cannot be now expected to be long.

Grant
O God
that I may no longer resolve in vain,
or dream away the life that thy indulgence gives me,
in vacancy and uselessness.

From the diaries of Samuel Johnson (1709–84)
(Entry for Easter Day, 30 March 1777)

Bruce Kent

'I don't know any short piece of writing that better expresses the insignificance of human beings, and yet their immense importance.'

Psalm 8, you could say, is a living paradox. It describes the trust which God has shown to humankind, when he has lavished on them glory, honour and power. His sovereignty is so wide that even the lips of babes and children proclaim his praise.

'Perhaps that is going a bit far if you take it literally. Children and babes are not reciting prayers. But in their presence and trust they reflect the amazing wonder of God. Through their presence comes the absolute mystery of their very existence, that what did not exist is suddenly there, with personality and life. Through their need for parental care, they exhibit a trust. And, of course, simple people are very often much closer to God than those who are very complicated, so in that sense I think those lines are correct.

'I share the psalmist's sense of wonder. It gives me humility. I don't know that I am naturally humble, but to realize that you have such a short span here, and that, in that time, you have to use the talents you have been given, induces a humility about your own position.'

Do you see yourself 'a little less than a god'?

'Especially and supremely in human beings, I see God working out his plan. He uses us and endows us with love, generosity, unselfishness, compassion, amazing gifts which do not come from carbon atoms or lumps of coal. They are little windows opening into God through human beings. We could be just a speck of dust, but we are not. We are endowed with something of his attributes.

'With that goes enormous responsibilities, and here is a crossroads in the psalm. To say "everything has been put under your feet" is a road to exploitation. But if you take the whole psalm, we are made stewards of God in the image of God. So creation, the world, animals, birds and the "fish that make their way through the waters" are not ours to exploit, but we are to them as God is to us.'

Bruce Kent. Chairman, Campaign for Nuclear Disarmament, 1987–90 (General Secretary, 1980–85; Vice-Chairman, 1985–7).

How great is your name, O Lord our God,
through all the earth.

Your majesty is praised above the heavens;
on the lips of children and babes
you have found praise to foil your enemy, to silence
    the foe and the rebel.

When I see the heavens, the work of your hands,
the moon and the stars which you have arranged,
what is man that you should keep him in mind,
mortal man that you should care for him?

Yet you have made him little less than a god,
with glory and honour you crowned him,
gave him power over the works of your hand,
put all things under his feet.
All of them,
sheep and cattle,
yes, even the savage beasts,
birds of the air,
and fish that make their way through the waters.

How great is your name, O Lord our God,
through all the earth.

Psalm 8
(For a different version of Psalm 8, see Kriss Akabusi, p. 8)

Bernhard Langer

'It's not easy, but that is what the Lord tells us to do.'

The champion faces the challenge with disarming control. He stares ahead thoughtfully, as he ponders quietly on Paul's apparently impossible command: 'Rejoice in the Lord always'.

'Many of the things the Lord tells us to do are not easy,' says the golfer, 'and it is always a big challenge. I suppose that is why Jesus was the only perfect man, and we are all imperfect compared with his standards. I have been growing more and more as a Christian in the last few years, and I try to spend time with the Lord whether things are going great or whether they are going badly. I have had my struggles in life as well as in my career, but I think what he means is that we should rejoice, knowing that we are going to have eternal life. That means so much more than whatever this little thing might be we are struggling through. Whether it is little or big, it is nothing compared to having eternal life or not having eternal life.'

Here, the challenge comes from St Paul, in a famous passage written to the Philippians which Bernhard Langer has found an inspiration to his faith. Yet with the language of challenge, it seems, comes a certain placidity, best expressed in Paul's own words to 'present your requests', but 'do not be anxious about anything'.

'I think we are far too anxious about everything. We have so many fears and anxieties in our lives which hold us back. I have learnt in the past, when I have tried to do everything myself, or to figure everything out myself, that there are some things I just cannot figure out. They are not under my control, but in the control of other people. So there is no point in my being anxious about things when I cannot control other people or their thoughts. I can only pray that they will handle a situation in a decent manner.'

Paul goes further in his advice to the Christians in Philippi, to focus firmly on pure, excellent and praiseworthy things. Is it not a fool's paradise to have eyes only for what is good?

'No. We have so much a tendency to look on bad things, and I think we ought to spend more of our time and energy looking at the good things which are worthwhile looking at. I think the only way to improve ourselves and our lives is to look at the positive things and to try to be better and more positive in the future.'

Bernhard Langer. German golfer. Tournament wins include: US Masters (1985; 1993); Dunlop Masters (1980); Australian Masters (1985); European Open (1985); Irish Open (1987); 14 tournaments worldwide between 1988 and 1993.

Rejoice in the Lord always.
I will say it again: Rejoice!
Let your gentleness be evident to all.
The Lord is near.
Do not be anxious about anything,
but in everything, by prayer and petition, with thanksgiving,
present your requests to God.
And the peace of God, which transcends all understanding,
will guard your hearts and your minds in Christ Jesus.

Finally, brothers,
whatever is true,
whatever is noble,
whatever is right,
whatever is pure,
whatever is lovely,
whatever is admirable –
if anything is excellent or praiseworthy –
think about such things.

Whatever you have learned or received or heard from me,
or seen in me –
put it into practice.
And the God of peace will be with you.

Philippians 4.4–9
(New International Version)

Lord Longford

By April 1991, the Gulf War is over. But such is the damage that misery, hunger, starvation and death will go on and on. What shocks the world next is the plight of the Kurdish people, who had risen against Saddam Hussein, only to find themselves driven from their land, and caught on the snow-topped hills on the borders of Iraq, without food or warmth. Hundreds of them died in those days and weeks. It is then that I meet Lord Longford, himself known for his campaign for social justice, particularly amongst prisoners. The passage he has chosen from the Gospel according to St Matthew seems to tie together the two areas of concern, though its message of judgement and division goes against the grain:

'I don't believe in division between goodies and baddies. No one can be less ready than I am to divide, and I don't believe Christ divides us in that way at all. I have chosen the passage because of the wonderful message: "So much as you've done it to the least of these my brethren, you've done it to me". Take the starving Kurds: "I was hungry" or "I was naked", that is the Kurdish people. So whether we look into prisons or whether we look at the Kurds, always we think of Jesus Christ there in every human being.'

From the surprise displayed by the righteous at their own good works, does it follow that such good works, carried out self-consciously, are not to be counted as truly righteous deeds?

'No. I think a lot of people carry out these acts self-consciously. If you devote yourself to mentally handicapped people in this country, or if you are now serving among the hundreds of starving Kurds, you know you are doing work for Christ. But I think a lot of humble people, unknown people, go about their ordinary business and do not think that they are doing anything special. So it does not follow that you do them in order to get to heaven. I don't say "if I visit him and make rather a long journey, this should do me some good in the long run". When you are actually confronted with a prisoner, you just see a fellow human being. It happens very seldom that you actually see Christ, but you believe he is there in every human being. Whatever they have done, however unattractive, impoverished, stricken, dying, only just born, Christ is there.'

Lord Longford. 7th Earl of Longford, since 1961. Chancellor of the Duchy of Lancaster, 1947–8; Minister of Civil Aviation, 1948–51; Chairman, the National Bank Ltd, 1955–63; Secretary of State for the Colonies, 1965–6; Director, The Help Charitable Trust, 1986.

He shall set the sheep on his right hand,
but the goats on the left.
Then shall the King say unto them on his right hand,

> 'Come, ye blessed of my Father,
> inherit the kingdom prepared for you from the foundation of
> the world:
> For I was an hungred, and ye gave me meat:
> I was thirsty, and ye gave me drink:
> I was a stranger and ye took me in:
> Naked, and ye clothed me:
> I was sick, and ye visited me:
> I was in prison, and ye came unto me.'

Then shall the righteous answer him, saying,

> 'Lord, when saw we thee an hungred, and fed thee?
> or thirsty, and gave thee drink?
> When saw we thee a stranger, and took thee in?
> or naked, and clothed thee?
> Or when saw we thee sick, or in prison, and came unto thee?'

And the king shall answer and say unto them,

> 'Verily I say unto you,
> Inasmuch as ye have done it unto one of the least of these my
> brethren,
> ye have done it unto me.'

Matthew 25.33–40
(Authorized Version)

Lord Mackay

Do you see yourself as a sinful person?

'Yes.'

I had expected a more guarded reply from the highest judicial officer of the land. I wait, but his answer is complete.

The question sprang from the Lord Chancellor's choice of three verses from Psalm 51, perhaps the most urgent of the penitential psalms written by David after his adultery with Bathsheba.

'I think it is very important to see that David has been guilty of a very serious sin. He was one who loved his Lord, but he had found himself in this very serious sin, and this psalm takes us very deep into his experience once he confronted sin. I believe that, through the psalm, and through the experience he had in the psalm, he was cleansed.'

Do you regard this as a personal prayer as well?

'Oh yes. I think that is what the psalms provide in many places. They contain a tremendously rich variety of prayers for all sorts of circumstances, and over the years I have found that whatever one's circumstances, there is always something that seems appropriate to them somewhere in the psalms. They provide prayers in the experience of the psalmist that are appropriate for our experience. I am very conscious of my own wrongdoing, deficiencies and failures, and I believe that salvation from them is in God and in his mercy, as spoken of in this psalm, and in the presence of his Holy Spirit, as spoken of in this particular prayer.

'The gift of the Holy Spirit, I believe, is central. It leads us into the scriptures, enables us to find food, comfort and guidance, light and liberty in the word. To talk of "renewing a right spirit within me" is to hope for a new, loving and obedient spirit, and that the sin which is now past will not be repeated.

'I seek to use prayer continuously as a source of guidance. The scriptures say "pray without ceasing". That does not mean one is constantly actually praying, because one has work to do. But one seeks to carry on one's work in the spirit of prayer, asking for God's blessing on it, and his guidance, support and strength in it.'

Rt Hon. Lord Mackay of Clashfern. Lord High Chancellor of Great Britain, since 1987.

Turn thy face from my sins:
and put out all my misdeeds.

Make me a clean heart, O God:
and renew a right spirit within me.

Cast me not away from thy presence:
and take not thy holy Spirit from me.

Psalm 51.9–11
The Book of Common Prayer (1662)

Pat McCarthy

It is almost four and a half years since his son has been taken hostage in Beirut, when I first meet Pat McCarthy. He sees no escape from the extraordinary test of endurance which has overtaken his life. Waiting is mixed with almost impossible uncertainty. Pat knows that John will never see his mother again. She has died during his years as hostage, and Pat himself has changes to make in his life following her death. Yet he believes he must wait until after John's release. There is no guarantee that day will ever come.

The prayer of Sir Francis Drake measures endurance against achievement. But what of this special case when the end is so uncertain, or there seems to be no end?

'It is strange that there is no end. My marriage in one sense has ended because my wife has died, and yet I don't feel completely that it has ended. It is still as if, in some way, she is around. In the same way the "project" or task of the last four and a half years has been to make efforts to do what one can to secure the release of my son John still held hostage in Beirut. It is very frustrating, because one cannot make proper efforts, but one does what one can. One prays for that, of course, and that is not yet concluded. His captivity and his humiliation and degradation still go on. When John was kidnapped in April 1986, one had no idea that he would be a prisoner for such a long time. There is this endlessness there, but, of course, there will come a marvellous day when he is free again.

'In my life there have been various undertakings given by God, which have been important but also enjoyable, for example my marriage, having sons, raising them, and so on. I believe that it is God's will that this is what we do. It is something you have to make a good job of, or at least you have to try.'

John McCarthy was released from captivity almost one year later, on 8 August 1991.

Pat McCarthy. Father of the former hostage, John McCarthy.

82

O Lord God,
when thou givest to thy servants to endeavour any great matter;
grant us also to know that it is not the beginning
but the continuing of the same until it is thoroughly finished
which yieldeth the true glory.
Through him who, for the finishing of thy work,
lay down his life for us,
our redeemer,
Jesus Christ.

Based on a saying of Sir Francis Drake

Edward Norman

On Midsummer's day 1537, two young men took their priestly vows in Venice. One was St Ignatius of Loyola, and the other was his friend St Francis Xavier. A few years later, Francis began his travels to the East which began his life of missionary work.

'St Francis Xavier was uncompromising about the importance of revelation, and about why Christianity needed to be brought to people who did not know Christ. He was concerned that the religions of the East should achieve our respect and understanding, but that they were not to be regarded as the ultimate dispensations of truth. The God who is known to Muslims, Hindus and Sikhs is the God who is truly God, because he is the God known through nature. But Christianity – revealed religion – is superior, because, in revealed religion, God is not just descriptively present in the world, but he actually brings salvation and forgiveness.'

The prayer demands an understanding of the nature of intercession for the faith of another person, who, though created in the image of God, is ignorant of his love. Are some people created more in God's image than others?

'No. The latency of God is present to all men and women, but this does not do anything in the procurement of salvation. People, as we try to respond to our religious understanding, need some active quality. This is the difference between being "made in God's image" and being "children of God". Then you receive the additional gift, which he gives, of forgiveness. If I were asked to define what the Christian Church is, I would define it as the company of people who are forgiven.'

It is also the company of people, according to St Francis Xavier's prayer, who are responsible for the prayers and labours which might bring deliverance from false belief and faith. But if God creates men and women, why does he need the Church, as a third party, to bring him together in love with the beings he has created?

'I don't think the Church is a third party. The Church is the people of God, and Jesus, in giving his new dispensation to mankind, did not confirm his truth in the form of words. He did not write a book. He gave his truth to a people. They were, as it happens, the common people who heard him gladly through the gospel. To this day, that body of people is the only reliable source of the authority of Christ's words. So we need to look around in the world to see who these people are.'

Revd Dr Edward Norman. Dean of Chapel, Christ Church College, Canterbury, since 1988; Dean of Peterhouse, Cambridge, 1971–88.

O God of all the nations of the earth,
Remember those who,
though created in your image,
are ignorant of your love;
and, in fulfilment of the sacrifice of your Son, Jesus Christ,
let the prayers and labours of your Church
deliver them from false faith and unbelief,
and bring them to worship you;
through him who is the resurrection
and the life of all who put their trust in you,
Jesus Christ,
our Lord.

St Francis Xavier (1506–52)

Christopher Patten

'I think he is the greatest Englishmen and the greatest of Saints.'

Chris Patten is admiring one of the most brilliant men of sixteenth-century public life. The Lord Chancellor of England, Sir Thomas More, canonized by Pope Pius XI in 1935, was beheaded by Henry VIII on 6 July, 1535.

'I think he exemplifies a lot of the qualities which I particularly admire and he is quintessentially English. Right to the moment of death, he was both joking as he ascended the steps to the scaffold, and asking those who were there to watch him be decapitated, to pray for Henry VIII.'

Much of that spirit penetrates the prayer, with its petition for mercy not only for the faults of all that harm him, but for the faults of his own as well. Is the twentieth-century politician so willing to throw himself in with those who oppose him?

'I think as a Christian, or with any religious belief, you have to do that in order to avoid becoming sanctimonious. There is a particular grace about recognizing one's own faults when standing out against other people's, or being harmed by other people's. I think all of us have a particular tendency to overlook our own inadequacies, and the more we are able to look at ourselves and examine our own failings, the better, without making us too negative or depressed. I think one needs to keep a balance when observing the way other people treat one in life.'

So does the stated desire to share paradise with those who have warred against him affect the way he sees them on earth?

'I think it must do, and I think it makes magnanimity, in both one's individual relationships and beyond, such an important and marvellous virtue. Almost my favourite painting is a painting by Velázquez called *The Surrender of Breda*, which hangs in the Prado in Madrid. The expressions on the faces of those who are shaking hands after the surrender is marvellously full of grace. I think that in personal relationships one has to show that same grace and balance, and recognize, as someone who believes in an afterlife, that, since you want it for yourself, you must want it for other people too.

'And however right you think you are in a given course of action, or however much faith you have in your own integrity, you should constantly question your own conduct and pray for those who you think are doing you harm. Because we can all be sure of one thing: we are all doing other people harm; we are all hurting other people, both people close to us and those further away.'

Rt Hon. Christopher Patten. Governor-General of Hong Kong, since 1992. Secretary of State for the Environment, 1989–90; Chairman, Conservative Party and Chancellor of the Duchy of Lancaster, 1990–92.

Almighty God,
have mercy on all that bear me evil will,
and would me harm,
and their faults and mine together,
by such easy, tender, merciful means,
as thine infinite wisdom best can devise,
vouchsafe to amend and redress,
and make us saved souls in heaven together
where we may ever live and love together
with thee and thy blessed saints,
O glorious Trinity,
for the bitter passion of our sweet Saviour Christ.

St Thomas More (1478–1535)

John Peters

On 17 January 1991, news came through that a British Tornado had been lost in the Gulf, after an attack on the Allies' second Tornado mission out of Bahrain. A few days later, the first two British prisoners of war were paraded on Iraqi television. The pictures were shown in Britain and worldwide. Later, the pilot of the aircraft, Ft Lt John Peters, publicly described the torture he and his navigator had received, something of which could be seen in those television pictures. Such were the feelings provoked by the pictures that literally thousands of cards were sent to him, his wife and family, mostly by people who knew nothing of him but as the victim of a single merciless act.

A year later John brings with him the words which so many wellwishers had passed on to him. Though hesitant to describe himself as a church-going Christian, he has been deeply impressed and aided by the words of the 'footprints' meditation.

'I know you get a lot of these passages in bookshops, but for me this one meant something, and it was written in simple words. It was not in the superlatives you tend to get in prayer books, and I think its meaning is clear but not simplistic.'

How were you affected by trial and suffering?

'My trial has been a very public trial, whereas lots of people go through bad times in their lives and cope with those situations without any major changes to their lives. I was in a situation where I did pray, and indeed all the prisoners of war prayed, having gone through my life not realizing that, when the time came, I would indeed turn to prayer.'

How strong was that at the time?

'Oh, it was pretty strong. It was a necessary part of the time I was in there.'

Does this poetical dream tally with reality?

'Yes. I go through life, and really God does not play a significant part of my life. I don't really go to church. But then I was put in a bad situation, and in fact I turned towards him. I think this passage includes people very much like myself, an agnostic, or even those who believe. You think that God should provide you with something when you have difficulties, but when the going really gets tough, you believe properly. And that does provide you with help, and he is there helping you.'

Ft Lt John Peters. RAF pilot; first hostage taken in war against Iraq; shot down 17 January 1991, with navigator John Nichol.

One night a man had a dream.
He dreamed he was walking along the beach with the Lord.
Across the sea flashed scenes from his life.
For each scene he noticed two sets of footprints in the sand,
one belonging to him and the other to the Lord.
When the last scene of his life flashed before him,
he looked back at the footprints in the sand.
He noticed that many times along the path of his life
there was only one set of footprints.
He also noticed that it happened
at the very lowest and saddest times in his life.

This really bothered him and he questioned the Lord about it.
Lord, you said that once I had decided to follow you,
you would walk with me all the way.
But I have noticed that during the most troublesome times in
    my life,
there is only one set of footprints.
I don't understand why,
when I needed you most you would leave me.

The Lord replied,
My son,
my precious child,
I love you and I would never leave you.
During your times of trial and suffering,
when you see only one set of footprints,
it was then that I carried you.

'Footprints'

Edward Pickering

The huge complex in East London which houses Times Newspapers makes an impressive showpiece for the printed word. Though the reporters' rooms, once rattling with hurried scoops, are silenced by the new technology, the printing presses are grander, faster and more powerful than ever before. The visitor, like myself, cannot fail to be impressed by the ingenious and improbable mechanics which are used to print, fold, bundle, pack and distribute thousands of copies of Britain's daily papers in time for the early morning round.

My guide is the Executive Vice-Chairman of Times Newspapers, Sir Edward Pickering. For him, the printed word has formed the basis of a professional life. It also nourishes his life of prayer.

'The written word can be a great expression for us of what prayer can be about. I take the view of prayer as being an encounter between ourselves and God, and the act of praying just eases open the door that enriches that encounter. In *The Book of Common Prayer*, which reminds us all the time of what has been written and what has been printed, we join in an expression of prayer which is traditional, extraordinarily valuable and inspiring. That, to me, is the importance of the written and printed word.

'One of the great advantages of having the English Bible and *The Book of Common Prayer* is that, for many of us, it provides not only a literary background but a store of phrases which are a permanent guide in our daily lives.

'Of course there are dangers of misinterpretation, but the exposition of the written and the printed word help us enormously to see all kinds of different aspects to what may be interpreted from those words.'

Turning from the word to the Word, I ask what the relationship is between the scriptures and God.

'It is spelt out for us in the opening of John's Gospel: "In the beginning was the Word, and the Word was with God, and the Word was God." It is a very profound thought. I don't think I could approach it and understand it without the written word, and even now, I have to refer to the written word to maintain my understanding of the Word.'

Sir Edward Pickering. Executive Vice-Chairman, Times Newspapers Ltd, since 1982; Managing Editor: Daily Mail, 1947–9; Daily Express, 1951–7; Editor, Daily Express, 1957–62; Chairman, Mirror Group Newspapers, 1975–7.

Blessed Lord,
who hast caused all holy Scriptures to be written for our learning:
Grant that we may in such wise hear them,
read, mark, learn, and inwardly digest them,
that by patience and comfort of thy holy Word,
we may embrace and ever hold fast the blessed hope of everlasting
life, which thou hast given us in our Saviour Jesus Christ.

Collect for the Second Sunday in Advent
The Book of Common Prayer (1662)

John Polkinghorne

'The psalms attract me as a scientist because they are rooted in experience; the experience of God, of his presence and of his absence. The psalmist often protests about God's absence, and it is that recognition of experience and search for understanding and coherence, amidst the perplexing problems of experience, that attracts me to the psalms. I have chosen this particular psalm because it is concerned with creation.

'People often think that it is only the first chapters of Genesis that are concerned with creation, but there is a great deal more about it in the Old Testament. Psalm 104 celebrates the fruitfulness of God's handiwork.

'The psalmist sees God clothed with majesty and wearing light as a garment. I have two visions of God: one is that he surrounds himself in glory in the sense that he is the great one who is the ground of all that is, and whose mightiness and power are shown in the vastness and beauty of his creation. But as a Christian, I also think of God as one who clothed himself with humility and humanity.

'The expressions of creation, "he maketh the clouds his chariots", and "ridest upon the wings of the wind", are concerned with a picture of God who is somehow active in the world. As a scientist, I am concerned to understand whether that is a possibility. Is the world so closed and so mechanical in its nature that really the best God could be would be a cosmic clockmaker? Actually I think the world is free and open in its processes. It is much more like clouds than like clocks, and that is how we are able to be free and active in it.

'It is a very exciting thing to see how wonderfully structured the world is, and how delicate. And the balance and fruitfulness of its forces, and the way that the world seems shot through with mathematics, speaks to me of a mind, or a Mind, behind that world. And the wisdom of the creator is manifest in the beauties of the law of physics.

'As a scientist I seek understanding, and I seek that also as a Christian believer, trying to make sense of the one world of our experience. Science is understanding particular aspects of the world, the physical process of the world and the structure that lies behind it. There are many other questions, of meaning and purpose, which science does not address, but which we have to ask about the world. So I see the scientific quest and the religious quest as being comradely related to each other, as both seeking understanding of the remarkable and rich world in which we live.'

Revd John Polkinghorne. President, Queens' College, Cambridge, since 1989; Professor of Mathematical Physics, Cambridge University, 1968–79.

Bless the Lord, O my soul!
O Lord my God, thou art very great!
Thou art clothed with honour and majesty,
who coverest thyself with light as with a garment,
who hast stretched out the heavens like a tent,
who hast laid the beams of thy chambers on the waters,
who makest the clouds thy chariot,
who ridest on the wings of the wind,
who makest the winds thy messengers,
fire and flame thy ministers.

O Lord, how manifold are thy works!
In wisdom hast thou made them all;
the earth is full of thy creatures.

Psalm 104.1–4, 24
(Revised Standard Version)

Jonathon Porritt

'He was a passionate environmentalist.'

The Director of Friends of the Earth claims a fellow campaigner in the poet Gerard Manley Hopkins.

'They didn't really have them in those days, but he was one, and he felt that part of his duty as a Christian was to take up the cause of the earth and argue it passionately in the way that he does.'

The argument comes in the form of a poem which puts a wearisome and flawed image of man's endeavours on earth.

'There are various bits in the poem that make an enormous amount of sense to me. He explains how we have become alienated from the earth, saying, "the soil is bare now, nor can foot feel being shod". What he is getting at is the fact that we are separated from the living earth, not just by our shoes, but by concrete and tarmac and steel, and all the artefacts of the built world that separate us from the living earth. And I think he was implying that unless we get in contact with the living earth, we cannot carry out our responsibilities as Christians.

'He says "all is seared (burnt) with trade", and if you look at the footprint of man on the planet, now trod in every last corner of the planet, I think it is fair to use that word in a rather harsh way. I don't think we have trod gently or lightly, and we have not found a way of living in harmony with the planet. We have burnt our way wherever we could in order to get out of the earth what we felt we needed. I think it is tough for a good reason, because we have basically abused and exploited the earth.

'I don't think we can sustain what we do not revere, and the thing that is missing in our approach to the nature world is that sense of reverence, that sense of involvement and that sense of protecting it as the servants of God.'

Jonathon Porritt. Director, Friends of the Earth, 1984–90; Chairman, Ecology Party, 1979–80, 1982–4.

The world is charged with the grandeur of God.
  It will flame out, like shining from shook foil;
  It gathers to a greatness, like the ooze of oil
Crushed. Why do men then now not reck his rod?
Generations have trod, have trod, have trod;
  And all is seared with trade; bleared, smeared with toil;
  And wears man's smudge and shares man's smell: the soil
Is bare now, nor can foot feel, being shod.

And, for all this, nature is never spent;
  There lives the dearest freshness deep down things;
And though the last lights off the black West went
  Oh, morning, at the brown brink eastwards, springs –
Because the Holy Ghost over the bent
  World broods with warm breast and with ah! bright wings.

'God's Grandeur'
Gerard Manley Hopkins (1844–89)

Enoch Powell

'When I come away after Holy Communion, I nearly always find that a phrase out of this prayer is echoing in my mind: "... and dost assure us thereby of thy favour and goodness towards us". By what has happened, I have been assured a favour and goodness towards me of the Creator.

'The great problem of humanity since it came into existence, with its self-consciousness of its life and death, of interminability of life and of the potential hostility of the universe around it, has been to find some means of believing that there is a goodness and a favourable aspect of the environment towards mankind. I think that human worship is a means of satisfying this craving for a universe which will not be hostile or separated from us by an unbridgeable gulf, but a universe in which the facts of life and death will be reconcilable with goodness. To be assured of goodness and favour towards us is the reassurance which Holy Communion gives.

'This gulf cannot be bridged by reason. It cannot be bridged by anything which we can do practically. It cannot be bridged by any scientific experience or by a drug. It can only be bridged by worship. It is only by people worshipping together that they can succeed in crossing the gulf and be assured of a favour and goodness towards them of a spirit which rules the universe. It is something which cannot happen otherwise than by a symbolic and collective act.'

Another phrase from the same prayer describes the communicant Christians as 'heirs through hope of thy everlasting kingdom'. Does the use of the word 'heirs' imply a right to the Kingdom of God?

'No, that is exactly what the legal draftsmen intended to exclude. Had they left out "through hope", an indefeatable right to the Kingdom would have been asserted. But Christians are heirs expectant, not heirs in possession, and they need hope and encouragement in the period of expectation.'

Rt Hon. Enoch Powell. Former Member of Parliament. Professor of Greek, University of Sydney, 1937–9. Brigadier in the Second World War. Financial Secretary to the Treasury, 1957–8. Minister of Health, 1960–63.

Almighty and everliving God,
we most heartily thank thee,
for that thou dost vouchsafe to feed us,
who have duly received these holy mysteries,
with the spiritual food
of the most precious Body and Blood of thy Son
our Saviour Jesus Christ;
and dost assure us thereby of thy favour and goodness towards us;
and that we are the very members incorporate
in the mystical body of thy Son,
which is the blessed company of all faithful people;
and are also heirs through hope of thy everlasting kingdom,
by the merits of the most precious death and passion
of thy dear Son.

part of a prayer from the Order for
Holy Communion
The Book of Common Prayer (1662)

Cliff Richard

Cliff won his first Gold Disc in 1959. There were four in the 60s, three in the 70s, five in the 80s, and so it goes on. There are films, concerts, television shows and books. Few people can command such box office appeal for so long. And perhaps few would see him as an ant on the face of the world. He does.

'The thing that has amazed me most is the love of God through Jesus Christ, that God can love an ant like me.'

The remark springs from a famous passage from Paul's letter to the Romans, with its defiant question 'Who shall separate us from the love of Christ?' So what is the bond Cliff knows?

'It is Jesus that bonds me to God. The funny thing is that it is more likely that we are going to separate ourselves from God than anything else. We are the ones who fall away. We are the ones that stop praying, or stop going to church or reading our Bibles. But what this is saying is that nothing will be able to separate me from God: not myself, or what I do or think, or what anybody else thinks or says about me. None of that is ever going to separate me from God.

'I have felt the pressure over the years, as a Christian in the public eye, that the knives are there. Sometimes you feel that the media would be happy to see you trip up. I have been belittled and derided thousands of times for what I believe. So in some respects there is a kind of persecution there, though the word "persecution" is so strong that I hardly want to use it about what happens to me. But by going back to the Old Testament, what Paul says in this passage is "Look, you are already warned that if you become part of God's family, this is what is likely to happen to you".'

Are the words 'we are more than conquerors' a warning against a triumphalist approach?

'We are triumphalists, but I feel you have to remain triumphant within yourself while available and untriumphant to the man who does not believe. There is nothing more off-putting than somebody who says "Hey, you are a sinner and I am a saved man, I am a winner." That is going to turn people off. We still have to approach people and say "I am not triumphant because I deserve my triumph. I am a Christian and accepted by God in spite of the fact that I do not deserve it, and that there are no greater sinners than me".'

Cliff Richard. Pop star and actor. Top Box Office star of Great Britain, 1962–3 and 1963–4; 13 Gold Discs, 1959–88; 33 Silver Discs; 2 Platinum Discs, 1981 and 1986.

Who shall separate us from the love of Christ?

Shall tribulation,
  or distress,
  or persecution,
  or famine,
  or nakedness,
  or peril,
  or sword?

As it is written,

> 'For thy sake we are being killed all the day long;
> we are regarded as sheep to be slaughtered.'

No, in all these things we are more than conquerors
through him who loved us.
For I am sure that neither death,
  nor life,
  nor angels,
  nor principalities,
  nor things present,
  nor things to come,
  nor powers,
  nor height,
  nor depth,
  nor anything else in all creation,
will be able to separate us from the love of God
in Christ Jesus our Lord.

Romans 8.35–9
(Revised Standard Version)

Robert Runcie

'The decade which is just coming to an end has been a turbulent one.'

The last interview of the 1980s is a chance to gather together the experiences of the past years, and take them forward into a new decade. Robert Runcie, who became Archbishop of Canterbury at the beginning of the decade, chooses the words of one of his predecessors, Thomas Cranmer, to aid him in this task. The collect, from an older Latin prayer, presents to God the unruly wills of sinful men, and yet asks for the will to love the things which he commands.

'He creates an order into which you enter, that not only enables you to be at prayer, but also nourishes and steadies you in faith, amidst so many changes by which we are surrounded.

'I think that somebody in a Graham Greene novel was described as "not so much a person, more a civil war", and I think we all have that element in us, the "unruly wills" of chasing after our own ambitions, of having moments of self-pity or moments that tempt us to cynicism and despair. So I find this a prayer which is personal, and yet it is not just selfish.

'It is funny to think that God's love for us, and his promise to be on our side in life, is what draws out the desire to fulfil his commandments, and that is something that I know, not just in myself, but also in others. And I am very struck that Cranmer brings together love, obedience and joy. These are three fundamental things. Love on its own is sentimental, obedience on its own can be too tough, and joy – true joy – comes not from those neat harmonies in life which produce happiness, whether good health or temperamental compatibility in a marriage, but it comes very often where things are askew. And where that which is askew is faced and seen through, comes something deeper, the joy that is spiritual and indestructible.'

Lord Runcie. Archbishop of Canterbury, 1980–91; Bishop of St Albans, 1970–80.

O Almighty God,
who alone canst order the unruly wills and affections of sinful men:
Grant unto thy people,
that they may love the thing which thou commandest,
and desire that which thou dost promise;
that so, among the sundry and manifold changes of the world,
our hearts may surely there be fixed,
where true joys are to be found;
through Jesus Christ our Lord.

Collect for the Fourth Sunday after Easter
The Book of Common Prayer (1662)

Deus qui fidelium mentes unius efficis voluntatis: da populis tuis id amare quod praecipis, id desiderare quod promittis; ut inter mundanas varietates ibi nostra fixa sint corda ubi vera sunt gaudia per Dominum.

Gelasian Sacramentary

Prunella Scales

'One of the best things about being an actor is that you frequently get the chance to say things in words written by other people, far better than any of your own would be; and that act of saying other people's words not only expands your thoughts but actually changes you as a person. Sometimes it changes you quite permanently, not just for the evening or for the duration of the play, and I think that can also be true of a classic prayer.'

This is one of them, a classic Latin collect, translated for Cranmer's 1549 Book of Common Prayer, and reworked by the authors of the later revision.

'I quite see that the clergy today need an alternative service book, and I am sure that God doesn't mind what words people use when they pray. But I like to hear Cranmer from time to time partly because, as all actors know, there is something exciting about repeating words that have been used for many generations. There is nothing more moving to me, for instance, than a modern Saturday night audience falling about at a four hundred-year-old joke!

'And some of the phrases that Cranmer uses in the prayer book are so original that they are not only a pleasure to use, but they change you. They change your thinking.'

The petition of the prayer is for 'such strength and protection, as may support us in all dangers, and carry us through all temptations'. What has carried her through danger and temptation?

She pauses.

'I don't think I can answer that. I don't think I am a person who has been exposed to extreme danger or extreme temptation, but I think that everybody knows that sense of being unable to stand upright, and I think it is something you can pray about. I never know what things you can pray for. I never know whether you can pray for rain, because rain is scientifically organized, and, although God can work miracles, it is a lot to hope that God will send rain when there is none on the horizon. But that God will support you and carry you through dangers and temptations, I think is something you *can* hope for and pray for.'

Prunella Scales. Actress. Television series include: Fawlty Towers, *1975, 1978;* Mapp and Lucia, *1985–6; After Henry, 1988, 1990.*

O God,
who knowest us to be set in the midst of so many and great
dangers,
that by reason of the frailty of our nature
we cannot always stand upright:
Grant to us such strength and protection,
as may support us in all dangers,
and carry us through all temptations;
through Jesus Christ our Lord.

Collect for the Fourth Sunday after the Epiphany
The Book of Common Prayer (1662)

*Deus qui nos in tantis periculis constitutos pro humana
scis fragilitate non posse subsistere: da nobis salutem
mentis et corporis ut ea quae pro peccatis nostris pati-
mur te adiuvante vincamus per Dominum.*

Geoffrey Smith

'You know that God made the world – you *know* that don't you?'

I wonder from the twinkle in his eyes what can be coming next. It's his version of creation.

'When God had finished all the rest he made the Lake District, and he paused for a minute and thought, "Well, I've almost had enough practice, now for the ultimate." Then he made the Yorkshire Dales, and he said "Right, that's perfect!"'

As he chuckles, he calls me over to a shrub in the garden.

'Come and look at this.'

I look down. Beneath the plant a little rabbit nibbles away. There is no hutch. There is not even a fence, but the rabbit has lived in the garden now for more than a year. Geoffrey Smith grins. He mentions these things again when we come to talk about his passage from St Mark, because they illustrate the way he understands Christ's teaching on children and the kingdom of God.

'You miss something when you become so sophisticated that you cease to be a child. I still stop, absolutely spellbound, when I see that view from the top end of Swaledale. I must have seen it hundreds of times, but I still stop and look, and suddenly I feel this acknowledgement to God, just for the sheer beauty of the world as it is.

'Yes, that's childish. I'm a big kid! That rabbit I showed you in my garden, that's a wild rabbit which I feed with peanuts and I haven't tried to tame it. I get an immense kick out of that.'

Jesus is very firm with his disciples. He tells them that anyone who will not receive the kingdom of God like a little child will never enter it. Does that teach more about children or about God?

'I suppose equal balance of both. Imagine being Jesus, with the pressure that fame, notoriety and expectation must have put on that man, and yet, even though he was being pressured by intellectual and powerful people who could have done him a great deal of good, he pushed them away, and said, "Let the little children come to me, for of such is the kingdom of heaven." And that gives childhood its proper place.

'Of course there are little monsters. I was a little monster. I used to get up in the middle of the night to go out and watch badgers. My mother couldn't understand it, and she was complaining bitterly to an old Dales farmer who said, "Nay, missus: horses, dogs and young lads, they're not worth raising unless they've got a li'le bit'o spirit." Kids have got spirit, and I wouldn't want it any other way. But Jesus had time to say, let them come to him. And that's why, to continue feeling important and precious in the eyes of God, you must preserve an element of that childhood attitude right through life.'

Geoffrey Smith. Gardener and television presenter. Superintendent of the Northern Horticultural Society's garden project at Harlow Car, near Harrogate, 1954–75.

People were bringing little children to Jesus
to have him touch them,
but the disciples rebuked them.

When Jesus saw this, he was indignant.
He said to them,

'Let the little children come to me,
and do not hinder them,
for the kingdom of God belongs to such as these.
I tell you the truth,
anyone who will not receive the kingdom of God like a little
child will never enter it.'

And he took the children in his arms,
put his hands on them
and blessed them.

Mark 10.13–16
(New International Version)

Donald Soper

For sixty years or more, Tower Hill and Hyde Park have played host every week to the remarkable open-air ministry of Lord Soper.

From all his rich experience, one prayer stands out as a prayer of special importance which he has prayed time and time again. It is a collect which comes at the end of the Communion Service in the Book of Common Prayer which prays for continual help to glorify the name of God in every deed. But in its opening petition to go before (prevent) us in all our doings, does Lord Soper see some decisions of conduct taken from him?

'No. I pray for the kind of action in which you seek to walk in the steps of one who has gone before you and shown you the way. Therefore, the essence of right action for me is to look for the footsteps of Jesus and put my own feet in them. To find them I am looking for the reaction that I feel when I think of my life and the responses that I have to make to the various challenges of the day, and recognize that I am in need of help. I recognize then that I want guidance for the processes of life which are difficult for me and in which I have the consciousness of failure. I am asking for the help that comes from a guide rather than a map. You can lose the map, and the map offers no description of where you are going. So I want not only the immediate footsteps of Jesus in which to put my own but the continuing guidance of Jesus all the way.

What are the 'works' in which God may be glorified?

'They are the result of recognition of and demand for a particular quality of life and behaviour pattern. Whether a believer in Christianity or not, all of us are conscious of the gulf that separates what we would like to be and what we are, or what we ought to be and what we actually do. In that regard it is the call to the noble, God-like life which I find in Christianity that is the requirement of this prayer.

'That is the life that God would have us begin on this planet. And eternal life is the perfection, continuation or fulfilment of that which begins on this earth in my daily life now, and I am concerned that what I do today should be related to this eternal purpose and should not be just a sequence of events.'

Lord Soper. Superintendent, West London Mission, Kingsway Hall, 1936–78; Past President of the Methodist Conference.

Prevent us, O Lord, in all our doings
with thy most gracious favour,
and further us with thy continual help;
that in all our works,
begun, continued, and ended in thee,
we may glorify thy holy Name,
and finally
by thy mercy
obtain everlasting life;
through Jesus Christ our Lord.

The Book of Common Prayer (1662)

John Spong

'My belief in god grows stronger every day.'

The controversial American bishop is not in his usual combative mood. He quietly reflects on a very personal prayer, used at every service he has conducted since 1955.

'There is this overwhelming sense of the reality of God with me. I find God in the desert, I find God in the heart of the city, in the wilderness and in the rapids. It is an inescapable presence.'

Jack Spong's prayer is that God will sustain his people through all the burdens of life.

'I don't believe that burdens are *removed* by faith. I think one has the courage to carry them. The reason this particular petition has resonated so deeply in my life is that I have carried some interesting burdens. I am the child of an alcoholic father who died when I was twelve years old, so I know what it means to live in that kind of anxiety, and even abuse. When my father died, my mother, who is not an educated woman, was left in abject poverty. For twenty years before my wife died, she was a mental patient; and then, for the last six years of her life she had cancer, and so I had both the physical disease and the mental disease in the same person. In the process of this, I was raising three daughters. So this prayer said to me, there is no burden you can ever have that will cause you to be alone. You know that you are not able to have those burdens released. Of course, I would pray for her healing. She was never healed. But I never felt that I was alone in the midst of dealing with any of those, either my father, or my mother, or my wife or even in the process of being, in effect, a single father for twenty years.'

What are the ties which bind you, and prevent you joining fully with God?

'In every human life you have a number of things tugging at you. I have to raise questions with myself all the time. Do I do what I do because I am convinced that that is the right thing to do and I don't mind the consequences, or do I enjoy the public role of being a controversial and newsworthy bishop? Do I study the way I study Holy Scripture because it feeds me on a deep and abiding level, or because I want to use it to demonstrate my superiority over someone who has not studied it so well? There are all kinds of ego struggles that every human being goes through and that you know are separating you from the love of God. As Kazantzakis said in his great novel, "Sometimes you find you have done the right thing, but you have done it for the wrong reason". Part of my own spiritual life and development is to analyse my own motives over and over again, and to pray that finally there is only one tie that I am not willing to break. That is the tie that binds me to the gracious love of God.'

Rt Revd John Shelby Spong. Bishop of Newark, New Jersey, since 1976.

Gracious God

Send us anywhere in this world you would have us go,
only go thou with us.

Place upon us any burden you desire,
only stand by us to sustain us.

Break any tie that binds us
except the tie that binds us to thee.

And the blessing of God,
Father,
Son and
Holy Spirit
be with you now
and for evermore.

David Steel

The whole world was shocked. The Chinese government had done the unthinkable, and brutally murdered the students who mounted their peaceful protest in the now-famous Tiananmen Square. A few days after that horrifying event, I am to interview the former Liberal leader at the House of Commons. His prayer is one whose petitions reflect the international concerns of the moment, but whose origin brings back personal memories too. As a television interviewer in the 1960s, the Church of Scotland Moderator's son had interviewed Professor Barclay for a religious programme. A quarter of a century later, the memory of that encounter remains.

'He was one of the most erudite of biblical scholars in the Church of Scotland, but at the same time he had a remarkable facility for explaining texts. To hear him preach, or to hear him lecture, was a real experience, and this prayer itself is very simple in its language, and yet it retains beauty.'

Simple though it is, the prayer offers much to discuss, from the nature of the qualities needed in testing conditions, to the way in which they may be reflected in the one who prays for them. It is a prayer which recognizes earthly and heavenly values together. But is it possible to direct ambition towards both heaven and earth?

'I hope so. I think I have always regarded myself as a practical Christian, and I think that those who are concerned exclusively with the preservation of themselves and the life hereafter, and are not concerned with the application of Christ's teaching on earth, are really missing out on half of what Christianity should be.

'I think the qualities in the prayer are all those that people in public life or stressful situations ought to have. One of the situations which is uppermost in my mind is the sight of that Chinese student single-handedly trying to stop a procession of tanks, and I think that in situations like that you need every possible kind of help, guidance and sustenance. That is one of the references of the prayer. The other is control over oneself. Particularly in politics, it is so easy to be bad-tempered, intemperate or to lose control over your feelings on things, and I think that this is a prayer directed to try and save us from doing that.

'I hope for the qualities which come in the pursuit of justice. To use the phrase from one of the psalms which was used at the ecumenical conference at Basle, "may justice and peace embrace one another". I think the pursuit of those qualities in the nitty-gritty of policy-making would be reflecting what Christ was trying to teach us.'

Rt Hon. Sir David Steel. Liberal Democrat Member of Parliament; Leader of the Liberal Party, 1976–88; Co-founder, Social and Liberal Democrats, 1988.

O God, our Father, help us all through this day so to live that we may bring help to others, credit to ourselves and to the name we bear, and joy to those that love us, and to you.

    Cheerful when things go wrong;

    Persevering when things are difficult;

    Serene when things are irritating.

Enable us to be:

    Helpful to those in difficulties;

    Kind to those in need;

    Sympathetic to those whose hearts are sore and sad.

Grant that:

    Nothing may make us lose our tempers;

    Nothing may take away our joy;

    Nothing may ruffle our peace;

    Nothing may make us bitter towards anyone.

So grant that through all this day all with whom we work, and all those whom we meet, may see in us the reflection of the master, whose we are, and whom we seek to serve. This we ask for your love's sake.

William Barclay (1907–78)
(Sometime Professor of New Testament,
University of Glasgow)

Roy Strong

'I am a Christian who belongs to the Catholic tradition within the Church of England, and, for anyone who belongs to the Catholic tradition, the Eucharist, or Mass, is always central. This prayer comes right at the very end, and one goes out renewed, with a spring in one's step, happy and joyful. It took me a long time to learn about Christian joy. I can remember a priest saying to me, "You have not got much joy out of this." I thought about that, and found there was too much agony and not enough ecstasy. So I re-read the gospels, and that word "joy" keeps turning up. That was a tremendous turning-point for me, and the Christian faith has given me the most wonderful sense of joy.'

The prayer of which he speaks is the second of two post-communion prayers included in the Alternative Service Book. The first echoes the opening sentence of the thanksgiving prayer from the 1662 Book of Common Prayer (chosen by Enoch Powell,   p. 97). What sort of 'nourishment', I wonder, do the body and blood of Christ mean for Sir Roy?

'It is a symbol of union, love, sacrifice, repentance, hope and resurrection. Here every line in life suddenly converges, and it does not matter how far we have fallen, we know that there will be open arms there to receive us, and that we will never go away without feeling forgiven, uplifted, and endowed with a feeling of God's real love towards us. It is a great mystery, and it must be extraordinary to people who don't know anything about it, or who feel that they cannot be moved by that.'

The second sentence is drawn from the 1662 prayer of oblation which offers the idea of our souls and bodies as a lively (or 'living') sacrifice.

'You *are* a living sacrifice. Everything about you is animated by service to God, and therefore you live out that sacrifice. The whole of Christian living is made up of alternatives. With God's grace, you hope to go the right way, but that often takes a very heavy toll. What is wonderful is that if you take the wrong one, and I have many times, he is always there with outstretched arms, waiting for you to come back. That is beautiful; and I am grateful indeed for that wonderful sacrament of reconciliation.'

The final sentence reflects in mirror image the opening words of the Communion service: 'The Lord is here, his Spirit is with us', as it returns to the theme of the Holy Spirit, with the words 'send us out in the power of your Spirit'.

'I go out, having said that, thinking of all the things that I am involved in, and all the people who will be tied into those projects, and how I must think, in the power of the Spirit, about everybody and every aspect of that particular work. When the work is done one gives thanks for it, because it is the Spirit that sees you through.'

Sir Roy Strong. Writer, historian and lecturer; Director, Victoria and Albert Museum, 1974–87.

Almighty God,
we thank you for feeding us
with the body and blood of your Son Jesus Christ.
Through him we offer you our souls and bodies
to be a living sacrifice.
Send us out
in the power of your Spirit
to live and work
to your praise and glory.

The Alternative Service Book 1980

David Suchet

Interviewing actors can be disconcerting. Even friends sometimes mix the man with his character role. So interviewing David Suchet, I half expect to meet Hercule Poirot, Agatha Christie's famous detective, as he has become known to me through the popular television drama. The real David Suchet is very different. No tiny mannerisms, no Belgian tongue or irritating little walk. Instead, there is a confident and welcoming smile, and an infectious and bubbly enthusiasm for the Christian faith. He has chosen a passage from the Gospel according to St John, often associated with the feast of Pentecost:

'It is Jesus on a one-to-one with his disciples, promising the Holy Spirit which will come, but talking not just of the needs of the twelve or of the local community, but about his concern for the whole world.'

Do you find it disappointing that Jesus, describing himself as a spent force, places future hope elsewhere?

'No, I don't find it disappointing. I find it very optimistic. Jesus knew that his time as a man was rapidly coming to an end. He could no longer be with them in his own form. But we know that Christ was with God when the world began, and by going away he was able to send his Spirit to us, part of the triune God. And it is through his Spirit that he can stay with us until the end of time. So I find it very optimistic. It is our problem to tap into that.'

Do you ever feel that you know which way to go, but you don't understand why?

'Yes. I don't understand things nearly all the time. But I think that there is always the referral point to an inbuilt knowledge with us through the Holy Spirit, convicting us continually of our knowledge of what is right and wrong, irrespective of our education or anything else. And I have to be very careful that I am listening to the right voices. I have to check them continually, or, as Paul tells us, to "test the spirits". We have to test that what we hear is good, and of God. If we pray and listen to God our Father, and read the Bible, then we are going to be on safe ground.'

David Suchet. Actor. Television roles include Agatha Christie's Hercule Poirot, 1989. Best Actor, RTS, 1986.

It is for your good that I am going away.
Unless I go away, the Counsellor will not come to you;
but if I go, I will send him to you.
When he comes, he will convict the world of guilt
in regard to sin and righteousness and judgement:
in regard to sin,
because men do not believe in me;
in regard to righteousness,
because I am going to the Father, where you can see me no longer;
and in regard to judgement,
because the prince of this world now stands condemned.
I have much more to say to you,
more than you can now bear.
But when he, the Spirit of truth, comes,
he will guide you into all truth.
He will not speak on his own;
he will speak only what he hears,
and he will tell you what is yet to come.
He will bring glory to me by taking from what is mine
and making it known to you.
All that belongs to the Father is mine.
That is why I said the Spirit will take from what is mine
and make it known to you.

John 16.7–15
(New International Version)

Donald Swann

'Do you mind if I sing the prayer?'

This was a first for me, but I was pleased to telephone studio bookings and ask whether they would mind providing a piano for our interview. 'For *Prayer for the Day*?' 'My guest would like to sing his prayer!'

This is a prayer which Donald Swann has chosen for an interview to be broadcast on Armistice Day. He had already set it to music with a simple tune.

'It is the only prayer that I know that links private and public lives. It was used to help the United Nations Special Disarmament Programme in 1982. Mother Teresa was in St James's Church, Piccadilly introducing it, and her words were, "When I gave some rice to somebody who hadn't had any for months, that lady gave it to somebody else." That, she said, is neighbourliness, that is peace. So I see it as linking the personal and the public. There was a very public person saying "peace is right between me and my next door neighbour", especially the sick and poor person.

'On Armistice Day, I think one has to believe that there is a possibility of turning from armaments to food, and one just has to believe it. It is ever so difficult to do. And the falsehood is the world we have to live in. We just cannot bear to say goodbye to our defence systems and say, we give you this as grain.'

Have you ever made the transition from hate to love?

'Yes. Quite often. It is the most miraculous thing in life, and to some extent it is the foundation of my belief in the positive universe. As a Quaker, we think of Christ in every man, so it enables you to look your enemy in the face and say "Thank you for that Christ in you". That is a bit of a shaker. (A Quaker with a shaker!)

'This morning peace feels like an absence of war. But I can see a universal Armistice Day. I think we have a right to believe that we can end our particular wars, like the cold war or the war against famine. I think we could end that one in triumph. I think it can be done, and I think we have go to work for it.'

Donald Swann. Composer and performer; with Michael Flanders sang and accompanied own songs: At the Drop of a Hat, *1957, (two-year London run, Edinburgh Festival, Broadway, 1959–60).*

Lead me from death to life,
    From falsehood to truth;
Lead me from despair to hope,
    From fear to trust;
Lead me from hate to love,
    From war to peace;
Let peace fill our hearts,
    Our world,
    Our universe.

Satish Kumar,
adapted from the Upanishads

George Thomas

'Oh, it's only me,' says a lilting Welsh voice on the ansaphone at the BBC, 'it's only me, George Thomas.'

The message confirms a meeting with the man long known as Mr Speaker, who had judged the proceedings of the House of Commons from 1976 to 1983. The warmth and certainty in his voice are qualities which cannot be transcribed, but through them his every word is filled with infective confidence and power.

George Thomas has chosen a prayer by St Teresa of Avila, which bids the compassion and blessing of Christ. The challenge that 'Christ has no body now on earth but yours' can be taken two ways. Does it reflect the membership of the Church of Christ, or is it to be used as a message of personal responsibility?

'I see it both ways, first because, in the Communion Service, we say "we are now one body because we have eaten of one bread". But I also see it as symbolic that people everywhere who love the Lord Jesus Christ are committed, as one person, to a view of the world which is individual. We regard every person in terms of their possibilities, and I believe that when Jesus touches the human heart he transforms people, and their attitudes to life are changed. So the test of our faith is in how we live, in our attitude to other people and our attitude on great social issues. In short, it is to look at the world through the eyes of Christ.

'Compassion is to enter into the suffering of the person with whom you are dealing. We cannot close our eyes to suffering, because that is one of the few things the Lord could not do. He could do most things, but he could not pass by anyone who cried out in need. He had to stop and deal with them before he went on with his friends, and I believe that that is our mission too.

'I have been blessed in times of great stress in my life. In bereavement, when my heart has been heavy, and in every trial, even when I was Speaker of the House, I have been able to talk with Jesus. I hope people will not think I am wearing my heart on my sleeve when I say so, because it is so personal. But we have to have a personal relationship with our Lord before it becomes an all-consuming fire within us and takes us over. People can laugh at us if they like and claim that we are fooling ourselves or that life is an accident or chance. I don't care what they say. I know the Lord (and I *do* know him), and this prayer calls on us to be witnesses in the 1990s for Christ the Lord.'

Lord Tonypandy. Speaker of the House of Commons, 1976–83; Labour Member of Parliament, 1945–83; Secretary of State for Wales, 1968–70; Vice-President of the Methodist Conference, 1960–61.

Christ has no body now on earth but yours;
no hands but yours;
no feet but yours.
Yours are the eyes through which
is to look out Christ's compassion to the world.
Yours are the feet with which he is to go about doing good,
And yours are the hands with which he is to bless us now.

St Teresa of Avila (1515–82)
Spanish Carmelite nun and mystic

Jim Thompson

The seventy-sixth Bishop of Bath and Wells is about to be enthroned. The first bishop, a monk of Glastonbury, had gone to Wells in 909. So when Jim Thompson knocks on Wells Cathedral door in a few hours' time, and formally takes on the spiritual needs of his diocese, he steps into a job which has existed for a thousand years or more.

'When you take on a job like this,' he explains, 'you know that prayer is absolutely the heart of the thing.'

In the course of the enthronement service comes a prayer by one Thomas Ken, who was Bishop of Bath and Wells from 1685 until he was deprived from the see in 1690. It is a prayer for the grace and ability to pray, and it is this prayer that the Bishop brings to the radio audience too.

'Prayer is very difficult. Lots of people think they can't pray, like they can't draw or they can't paint. They say "I can't pray." But prayer is really about you and God, and it begins in the most simple conversations of the mind. You often don't feel the influence of prayer in your life straight away. I do not often feel "Oh gosh, God is standing right by me, and I have got to have an immediate conversation with him." It is much more like what the psalm calls "being planted by a watercourse", so that the roots go down beneath the ground and then they go out into the water, and they draw on that strength, and then the tree grows. So you don't often see the relationship between these prayers which you battle away with and the growth that is taking place.'

Do you call on God 'at all times'?

'Yes, I do. But I think it only comes in the *whole* of your life because you put it in very specific places in your life. I find that if I pray my half hour every morning then prayer is in my whole life. If I don't pray my half hour, when I am solely there for God, then I find that prayer does not spring up in the rest of my life so much. So to people who say that they pray all the time I would say, "Wonderful, if you have got to that stage, then you are near to heaven", but for me, and I think for most people, we need this special time of concentration on prayer.

'The same is true of church-going. People say "I don't need to go to church to pray." This is one of the great English fallacies, because you get your love of prayer, and your love of God, through sharing with other people who pray. They give your prayer validity, because you are with them, and you are joining in a great river of prayer without which I certainly could not go on.'

Rt Revd Jim Thompson. Bishop of Bath and Wells, since 1991; Bishop of Stepney, 1978–91.

Thou, O heavenly guide of our devotion and our love,
by teaching us to pray
hast showed us that prayer is
our treasury
    where all blessings are kept,
our armoury
    where all our strength and weapons are stored,
the only great preservative
and the very vital heat of divine love.

Give me grace to call on thee at all times by diligent prayer.
Lord, I know my devotion has daily
many unavoidable and necessary interruptions,
and I cannot always be actually praying.
All I can do is to beg of thy love,
to keep my heart always in an habitual disposition to devotion,
and in mindfulness of thy divine presence.
As thy infinite love is ever streaming in blessings on me,
O let my soul be ever breathing love to thee.

Bishop Thomas Ken (1637–1711)

Rick Wakeman

'I discovered this prayer by accident. I was doing some recording which required some devotional lyrics and which meant I had to choose some prayers, so I got the old Book of Common Prayer out and another book just called *Famous Prayers*, and I thought to myself, "This won't take me too long, a swift evening having a look through those . . . ." Unbelievable! I went through them hunting for weeks!'

What he found was a prayer he describes as wonderfully pertinent to his own situation, as he begins to look back over his twenty-five years as a leading rock musician. For a moment he looks away and smiles a little as he remembers the success and failure of his early career:

'Way back in the 70s, I was given wealth. But I was also given the "talent" – call it what you like! – to get rid of it very quickly, and at the end of the day I sit here now a wiser and a happier man. I wouldn't say I craved to have lots of money (and I haven't got it any more), it just appeared, and I was totally unprepared for it and didn't know what to do with it, just like some women are given beauty and don't know what to do with that.

'We should all be satisfied with our lot, grateful for whatever gift we've been given, however tiny and however small, and sometimes we can be given something, or sent something, that we think, "Oh, this is desperately unfair, I don't want this." But if you look into it, there is a meaning, and that's what makes this prayer so clever for me.'

We carry on talking for a while, straying from the subject a bit, to talk about his family life, the way his life has changed, and about the music he's playing on his six-week British tour. It all leads him back to the prayer.

'I genuinely do feel that I am much cared for and, for me, certainly my unspoken prayers are answered. When you accept the Lord into your life, and you accept Christianity wholeheartedly, that is the initial stage of tuning in, and that is when you start to understand a lot more things. That is when people's lives open up an awful lot more.'

Rick Wakeman. Rock musician. Top keyboard player and composer. Former Yes and Strawbs keyboardist. Early solo albums include: The Six Wives of Henry VIII, Journey to the Centre of the Earth. *Film scores include:* Lisztomania, The Burning, G'Ole, Crimes of Passion. *First Christian Album:* The Gospels.

I asked for strength that I might achieve:
I was made weak that I might learn humbly to obey.

I asked for health that I might do greater things:
I was given infirmity that I might do better things.

I asked for riches that I might be happy:
I was given poverty that I might be wise.

I asked for power that I might have the praise of men:
I was given weakness that I might feel the need of God.

I asked for all things that I might enjoy life:
I was given life, that I might enjoy all things.

I got nothing I had asked for
but everything that I had hoped for.

Almost despite myself
my unspoken prayers were answered.

I am, amongst all men,
most richly blessed.

Bernard Weatherill

'Hardly anything in life is absolutely black or absolutely white, and certainly that is true of politics. It is "on-balance" decision.'

As Speaker of the House of Commons, Bernard Weatherill sits daily as judge of the proceedings of the Commons, ensuring even-handed debate which is part of democracy itself. Curiously, for a life spent at the centre of the country's busiest debating chamber, life can be lonely, with few to turn to in the face of the most difficult decisions.

'Every night, before I go to sleep, I commit my problems to God. And every morning, just before I rise, I seek to obtain the answer by prayer. Very frequently it does happen overnight. If you commit your problems in a quiet, serene way to God, you often get the answer in the morning, although very frequently, I have to say, it comes when one is shaving, or having a last cup of coffee before going into the office, or maybe I am walking to the chamber.'

Turning to the prayer often known as the 'serenity prayer', I ask him about two key words. 'Serenity' is the first.

'I like to go back to the origin of words, and "serenity" comes from the Latin *serenus*, which means "clear" or "bright". And what I like to achieve is a clear indication of whether we have to accept this situation or that situation.'

And 'courage?'

'For me there are two forms of courage: there is physical courage, which we have tried to obtain in wartime, for instance, or certainly on the playing fields (but I am too old to play things these days). But there is also moral courage, and the one thing I learnt from my five years in the war is that, like it or not, you have to do your duty. And so to me it is very much a matter of moral courage to face up to problems that we have to face on a day-to-day basis, and also to seek to change things that can be changed. That often requires courage too. In my case the courage comes from my daily meditations, both in the evening and the morning. You could say, bluntly, from God.'

Rt Hon. Lord Weatherill. Speaker of the House of Commons, 1983–92. Conservative Member of Parliament, 1964–83.

God
grant me the serenity
to accept the things I cannot change,
the courage
to change the things I can
and the wisdom
to know the difference.

Reinhold Niebuhr (1892–1971)

Mary Whitehouse

'This is where it all happens.'

The centre of the most famous campaign against indecent and violent programming on television and radio is a single room in Mary Whitehouse's charming home, situated in a tiny village in Colchester. Though files stretch back to 1965, when the campaign began, this is no museum. It is the pitch for current battles and many more to come. Since the early days, even her own name has been adopted into the jargon of taste and decency talk. Her prayer reflects the battles:

'It touches very much the kind of life I live. Not only is it full of action, but it is also the kind of life that, when you get up in the morning, the shape of the day and what happens in it is still a mystery.'

The prayer offers her to God as a 'reliable tool' to be used 'without permission'. Does that make God a manipulative God, or one who offers no choice?

'I don't think "manipulative" in the way the word is generally used. I think that if one says to the Lord "I am here: if you want to use me, use me" he then knows that I am available to him for whatever he may want. But that is not to say I am always conscious that what I am doing is necessarily how the Lord would have me do it. Not by any manner of means. I think there is often a big gap between how one does respond to the kind of commitment one has made, and how ideally one should respond.

'What the prayer does say, in effect, is that there is no limit to what I would do, in principle anyway. And one of the things that I have learned, as I imagine many people learn as they get older, is that if you really have given your life to God and made yourself available to him, he will use mistakes, or things which seemed unfortunate at the time. That has been a very great comfort to me through the years.

'The campaign in which I have been involved has had a tremendous amount of attack centred on it, and perhaps on me personally. At first I found that very difficult; so there is no assurance that life is going to be comfortable. But, on the other hand, if you are prepared to go right in where the battle is being fought, you get lifted beyond your own capabilities. But if you go and do something in your own strength, something is going to go wrong, and the thing is not going to be what the Lord intended. So I think one has to be fearless, but at the same time trusting, so that you are not fearless in your own strength but fearless in the Lord's strength.'

Mary Whitehouse. President, National Viewers' and Listeners' Association, since 1980; Hon. General Secretary, 1965–80.

Keep me, Lord,
very close to you,
that I may be that homely tool on which you can rely
and which will not let you down.

Lord, I would be your hands in action,
your reliable tool,
As near to you as the sword is to the soldier
or the prayer book to the one who holds it.
I would that you could rejoice in me
and use me without first having to ask my permission
or fearing that my susceptibilities might be wounded.
Keep me near you,
so that I may discover
that it is indeed very good to be your child.

Pierre Charles

Shirley Williams

'I think this is somewhere near the heart of the problem of understanding the nature of God. A force that, at one and the same time, rules over these immense phenomena, and yet is capable, through his appearance in his Son, of producing somebody who relates so completely to other human beings, who lives like other human beings, and who does not set himself above them. That seems to me to get very near the heart of what one has to try to understand about the Christian gospel. I don't deny its difficulty. It is infinitely difficult. But it is also infinitely rich and worthwhile pondering upon.

'If I can put it in very human terms, it is one of the things that often happens to people in power, in the small-scale secular power that we politicians talk about. They become convinced of their own excellence, and become caught up in the first great sin of pride. After a while, they stop listening. They are unable to be reached, and become encapsulated in a world of their own.

'The crucial thing to me about this prayer, with its astonishing evocation first to the master washing the feet of his disciples on Maundy Thursday, and secondly as someone who girds himself in a towel, is to say that God is approachable. We can understand and reach him on a human level, even though his power, as the divine creator of the universe, is something we cannot fathom.

'You do not understand anything if you do not understand the astonishing, infinite power of the Almighty. But there is a balance in this prayer between that power, and an extraordinary capacity to hold back on the power, and to ask that the lessons of love, not of power, should dominate and shape human existence.

'The amazing thing about God is that he did not use his power to make human beings into those who would love and praise him without any question of choice throughout their lives. He allowed them to choose. And that itself was to accept a degree of humiliation from every human being who decides that his choice will be to reject God and to reject Christ.'

Baroness Williams. President, Social Democratic Party, 1982–8; Labour Member of Parliament, 1964–79; Secretary of State for Education and Science, 1976–9; Co-founder, Social Democratic Party, 1981.

The Wisdom of God
that restrains the untamed fury of the waters that are above the
   firmament,
that sets a bridle on the deep
and keeps back the seas,
now pours water into a basin;
and the Master washes the feet of his servants.
The Master shows to his disciples an example of humility;
he who wraps the heaven in clouds girds himself with a towel;
and he in whose hand is the life of all things
kneels down to wash the feet of his servants.

Maundy Thursday, Mattins
(Orthodox tradition)

Gordon Wilson

Suddenly, Enniskillen was a national landmark. When the Remembrance Sunday procession was sabotaged by a terrorist bombing attack in which eleven people were killed, chaos and grief hit the town. The world's media followed close behind.

People in Northern Ireland have become accustomed to terrorist attacks. But this one stood out. Among the victims of the killing was a twenty-year-old nurse called Marie Wilson, who managed to utter her final words "Daddy, I love you" before she died. A few weeks after the bombing, the Queen, in her Christmas message, remembered the words of forgiveness Marie's father, Gordon, had spoken on the day of the bombing, words which provided inspiration and hope for millions who heard them.

Five years have passed since then, but Gordon Wilson clings on still to the words of love which Marie spoke to him just before she died, and which he spoke of her killers soon after. He points to Jesus' teaching on love recorded by St Matthew as his source of inspiration.

'From day one in my life until right now, the word "love" is the word that keeps coming through; God's love for me, and me for him. I don't have any doubt about God's love for me, and I know that in my moment of need, his love for me saw me through what was, by my standards and perhaps by any standards, a very traumatic personal crisis. And when that crisis came, God did not fail me.'

Christ's commandment is to love the Lord your God with all your heart, soul and mind. Can you apply your conscious and unconscious self in that way?

He pauses. 'I can but try. I am no saint. I am a sinner, and that is a good place to start. But I know enough about what God tries to teach me, through his book and through his gospels, that Christ died for me so that I might repent and love him the more. My faith is simple; God loves me, and I must love him.'

Can you apply the same love to your neighbours?

'In my situation in Northern Ireland, loving one's neighbour means not just loving my Protestant neighbour. It also commands me to love my Catholic neighbour. And also, and this is the hard bit, to love my terrorist neighbour, and, God knows, we have some of them. I am talking about guys who took out my twenty-year-old daughter and ten others, and now over three thousand people in twenty years. And, believe me, it is not easy to love those men. But, as I keep reminding myself, Christ died for them too, and they must repent and seek his forgiveness, as I must. This is not to say I have to like them. I don't like them. They are evil men. But I have no hatred in my heart. I could not sleep with hatred in my heart. I am helped by this commandment to love them.'

Senator Gordon Wilson. Father of Marie Wilson, who was killed in 1987 by a terrorist bombing in Enniskillen. Irish senator since 1993.

An expert of the law tested him with this question:

'Teacher, which is the greatest commandment in the law?'

Jesus replied:

'Love the Lord your God with all your heart
and with all your soul
and with all your mind.

This is the first and greatest commandment.
And the second is like it:

Love your neighbour as yourself.

All the Law and the Prophets hang on these two commandments.'

Matthew 22.35–40
(New International Version)

Derek Worlock

It is rare to find such a bond between a prayer and him who prays it. But my visit to Archbishop's House in Liverpool during December 1990 marks a quarter of a century of earnest and daily repetition of a single prayer. Twenty-five years before our meeting, the Pope had chosen Derek Worlock as a Bishop, and almost every night since then had he uttered the words of the twelfth-century Cistercian monk who became Abbot of Rievaulx in 1147.

'I became very conscious', says the Archbishop, 'of people doing difficult things because I had asked them to.'

St Aelred's prayer takes in the difficult things with a plea for tender protection and the guidance of the Holy Spirit in working out a life of service to God's people.

' "God's people" is a very wide term. It is not just for Roman Catholics or members of my Archdiocese, but for all God's creatures. He knows what is in my heart, and that I am trying through my prayer to support anyone with whom I have any connection in their fidelity.'

He thinks especially of the Liverpudlian soldiers preparing for war in the Gulf:

'If you asked them whether or not they wanted God's tender protection, I think they would say yes. But I am asking for his protection not only for those who are in danger from war, but for those who are in any way subject to danger and temptation. I want them to be conscious that they can call upon the Lord for help, and I want them given the grace and the strength to carry through God's will.

'Christ promised his disciples that he would give them the Holy Spirit, to strengthen them and be with them in the huge task which he was giving them. The task was to bring the good news of his resurrection to the whole world, and the same Spirit which was given to the disciples is amongst us today. Often, after a marvellous or inexplicable turn round of events, you go away and say "That took us by surprise, but somehow I felt the spirit was amongst us".'

Most Revd Derek Worlock. Archbishop of Liverpool, since 1976. Bishop of Portsmouth, 1965–76.

Thou knowest my heart, Lord,
that whatsoever thou hast given to thy servant,
I desire to spend wholly on your people
and to consume it all in their service.
Grant unto me then, O Lord my God,
that thine eyes may be opened upon them day and night.
Tenderly spread thy care to protect them.
Stretch forth thy holy right hand to bless them.
Pour into their hearts thy Holy Spirit
who may abide with them while they pray,
to refresh them with devotion and penitence,
to stimulate them with hope,
to make them humble with fear,
and to inflame them with charity.
May he, the kind Consoler,
succour them in temptation
and strengthen them in all the tribulations of this life.

St Aelred (1109–1167)
Abbot of Rievaulx

ACKNOWLEDGEMENTS

Extracts from the Authorized Version of the Bible (The King James Bible), the rights in which are vested in the Crown, are reproduced by permission of the Crown's Patentee, Cambridge University Press.

Extracts from *The Book of Common Prayer*, the rights in which are vested in the Crown, are reproduced by permission of the Crown's Patentee, Cambridge University Press.

Prayers from *The Alternative Service Book 1980* are copyright the Central Board of Finance of the Church of England and are reproduced with permission.

The prayer on page 25 is from *Prayers and Meditations of St Anselm*, translated by Benedicta Ward SLG, and is reproduced by permission of the publishers, Penguin Books.

The extract from *The Living Bible* on page 29 is reproduced by permission of the publishers, Kingsway Publications.

The poem on page 55 is reproduced by permission of the publishers, Bloodaxe Books.

The prayer on p. 57 is reproduced with permission from *The Alternative Prayer Book 1984*, The General Synod of the Church of Ireland, published by Collins.

The version of Psalm 8 on page 75 is from *The Psalms: A New Translation for Worship*, and is reproduced by permission of the publishers, Collins Liturgical, an imprint of HarperCollins Publishers Ltd.

The prayer on p. 111 is reproduced with permission, the Barclay Trustees.

The publishers and author have made every attempt to contact copyright holders for the use of the material in this book. If copyright material has been used inadvertently without permission, the publishers would be delighted to hear from those concerned.

INDEX
of authors and references to prayers